ARCHITECTURE
TO
CONSTRUCTION

and everything in between

Create your Dreams . . .
Enjoy the Process . . .
Love the Outcome . . .

Steven & Jenny

Hope you Enjoy!

Paul

Paul D. Rugarber, AIA, NCARB
Architect

Paul D. Rugarber, AIA, NCARB
PDRdesigns Architecture
www.PDRdesigns.com

Published by PDRdesigns Architecture.

ISBN: 978-1-979847-186

First Edition: November 2017.

GRATITUDE

I sit looking at my completed book with a smile on my face. It has been a long journey that could not have been accomplished without some amazing people in my life!

My mom and dad who believed in me from the beginning; I love you!

My four children, Samantha, Allyson, Joseph, and Julia have been patient and encouraging to me in all that I do and for that , Thank you and I Love You!

Denise, who has encouraged me and taught me the importance of communication! Thank you and I Love You!

Donna Maltese, for being on my same wavelength and pushing me, Thank you!

Anthony, for editing pictures and retaking pictures to make me happy, thank you for the talent you have brought to this project.

Jennifer, for putting up with my continual adjustments and keeping everything running smoothly, Thank You!

To all the adversity in my life, which has molded me into who I am, I am grateful to you!

TABLE OF CONTENTS

(Your map to the book)

Entry

Kitchen

Great Room

Family Room

Living Room

Dining Room

Office

Master Suite

Bedrooms

Bathrooms

Closets

MISSION

"If I'd asked my customers what they'd wanted, they'd have said a faster horse."

— Henry Ford

The mission of this book is to enlighten homeowners as to the steps and procedures necessary to complete a renovation or new home project. Since designing and building projects over the past 20+ years, I have continuously been asked the same questions from owners about what they should expect during the design and construction process. They want to know how it unfolds, what they need to do, and when decisions need to be made. My mission in writing this is to answer those questions before you, the owner, even have a chance to ask them! Together, we will take a look at everything that goes into planning and implementing your project so that you know what to expect, when to expect it, and who to turn to for help. One step at a time, we will build up your knowledge base to create a strong foundation of understanding and appreciation for all that goes into your next project and allow you to enjoy the process.

Don't misunderstand – you won't become a general contractor by reading this book, but you will find yourself more informed and educated about what you need to do and what you can expect others to do along the way. My favorite saying is, **"There are no problems, only solutions!"** Keep this in mind and repeat it frequently, especially when you find yourself overwhelmed with the challenges at hand. Other words of wisdom and advice will be sprinkled in this edition to keep you positive and excited throughout. This is not a book to be read once and put aside – you should be referring to it as often as you need to guide you along your path. Skip around in whatever order you please and read the chapters that apply to you at the time, then reread and keep it handy as a reference throughout the project.

I can't stress enough how important it is to know all the information that's available to you when you are about to embark on a major financial journey, such as an addition or construction of a new home. Reading this book before you begin your project will save you an enormous amount of money and time by simply understanding what needs to occur and when, so please share this book with your friends and family before they commence a project of their own.

In the words of legendary football coach Mike Ditka:
"Life is not what you want it to be. It is what you make it."

The same applies to Architectural projects – so let's make yours a stunning success that you will be proud of for years to come!

My goal is to help you

CREATE YOUR DREAMS,

ENJOY THE PROCESS,

LOVE THE OUTCOME!

PDRdesigns Waterfront New Home Design

INTRODUCTION

All Journeys Begin with a Single Step

At times, great journeys can seem daunting, but when they are broken down into manageable steps, they become enjoyable and exciting.

This idea was impressed upon me in 2001, the year I began training to run a marathon in Dublin, Ireland, to help raise money for the Arthritis Foundation. Although a bit apprehensive because I had never run a marathon before, I ended up meeting a lot of great people and truly enjoyed training and competing.

In the process, I discovered that marathons are not daunting when they are broken down into easy, manageable steps. On the first day of training, I did not run 26.2 miles; I jogged a couple of miles and then increased the distance each week by following the training plan they provided. In the end, I did finish the marathon and while it was challenging at times, the end result was worth all of the hard work I had put in.

> *Tell me and I forget, teach me and I remember,*
> *involve me and I learn.*
> — *Ben Franklin*

Your project is your marathon, and this book is your training guide. It starts with a single step in the right direction, and before you know it, each of these steps will add up to a successfully completed project! **Think big; start small.**

The above quote is a favorite of mine as it rings true for many of us. Many of us fear certain tasks in life to the extent that often we ignore them just to avoid doing them. However, nine times out of ten, the fear will go away as soon as we actually get started!

Many people are afraid of construction projects just because they don't know what to expect. With this book, you'll gain the insight and knowledge you need to make informed decisions about the process involved. In turn, this will help you handle the occasional surprise, leading to a more enjoyable overall process. By managing your expectations, you will be calmer and have the ability to focus on the project and the process rather than stressing about the unknown.

> *"Do that which you fear the most and the death of fear is certain."*
>
> — *Mark Twain*

Throughout my career, I have come to understand that the majority of problems and disagreements stem from *mismatched expectations* between clients and professionals – it might be you and your architect, you and your contractor, or even between your architect and contractor. Make sure you communicate with your construction professionals during every step of the project! It's their job to make sure you have a full understanding of the project during the entire process. A strong foundation of knowledge, trust, and communication is absolutely essential to a successful project, and the best way to ensure you have these components is to ask plenty of questions.

Anyone that is committed to providing a great product or service will gladly explain everything you wish to know. One stipulation is necessary: In the words of Pierre Trudeau, "The essential ingredient… is timing." Make sure you have these discussions prior to starting each phase of your project.

That said, I am a firm believer in educating yourself and questioning everything – yes, _everything_. As you gain insight and information, it's important to know who you're asking and whether they're qualified to answer knowledgeably. **Don't ask your next-door neighbor who watches a lot of HGTV – ask an expert.** Look online, consult your team of professionals, read a book, and remember there are always different ways to accomplish the same task. With the wealth of information available these days, you have the ability to educate yourself and obtain any information you may need to be fully informed about your project.

This book progresses from the "Daydream Stage" to the "Final Certificate of Occupancy", feel free to jump around and read ahead, afterall- this book was written to help you! They say knowledge is power, so let's get you empowered! **Now, let's take the first step.**

1 THE WHOLE PROCESS IN A NUTSHELL

"Fall in Love with The Process, and the results will come."

— Eric Thomas

Most clients that come in to my office have very little understanding of what is going to occur in a construction project. They have never been told what happens and in what order, which causes quite a bit of anxiety. To help alleviate this, I have put together this quick overview of how a typical project will unfold from start to finish. Not every project has all of these steps, but whether you are creating a new house or an addition, this list will give you a broad understanding of what is involved. Each of the parts in this chapter is broken out in further detail in the book for a more in depth understanding.

Every great project, big or small, is stemmed from an emotional response to something that you would like to change. For example, needing more space to grow your family, creating an open floor plan for ease of entertainment, or simply updating and creating a whole new look. Whatever your reasons for building or renovating, here are the steps that need to be taken.

1. Determine your likes and dislikes about your existing space/home.

2. Be clear about the goal you want to accomplish with your project.

3. Hire an Architect to start the design process. Interior designers and any other design professionals you would like to hire should be brought in at this stage as well.

4. Determine if there are site or zoning constraints to prevent this type and scope of project.

5. Hire a surveyor and site engineer if needed.

6. Hire a General Contractor to implement designs

7. Complete the design process with your Architect

8. Obtain final pricing from your General Contractor.

9. File for building permits with the town, starting with zoning and engineering permits first, and then progressing to the building department permits. (This is typically handled by your General Contractor, but in same areas your architect will do this).

10. Make selections for materials and finishes to be used if this was not done in the design stage. (This is generally an ongoing process during construction.)

11. Begin construction. Your General Contractor will move the project through the steps of:

    - Tree clearing and/or site work

    - Digging and pouring footings and walls

    - Framing of floors, walls, and roofs

    - Installing windows, roofing, and siding

    - Installing plumbing pipes, ductwork, and electrical wires

    - Installing insulation and gypsum board

    - Installing interior doors, trim, tile, and cabinetry

    - Painting

12. Obtain building inspections as needed throughout each of the construction steps in. These inspections will be scheduled and attended to by your General Contractor.

    • Appliance and Fixture Installations

13. Obtain the Final Certificate of Occupancy (CO). This will be done by your General Contractor.

14. Do a walkthrough of your project with your General Contractor for any punch list items to be completed. (These are items that are not 100% complete, or scratches/errors.)

15. Most importantly, Enjoy your new home!

Remember: A journey of a thousand miles begins with a single step. Don't be afraid to take that first step. For it leads to your destination!

Photo by PDRdesigns

2 PROJECT PLANNING & ORGANIZING

The planning of your house project can be exciting or frustrating, depending on how you approach it. I plan to get you to see the fun in it, along with excitement about the idea of seeing your dreams come to life.

It is important to think about what you want, but more importantly, you should examine and understand *why* you want it. What emotions come into play with this project and how will the finished project make you *feel*? The emotional component is absolutely crucial to the process – capture this and allow it to become your vision that drives you each day! Dream a little, focus on those positive emotions, and get ready to believe in the possibilities!

There are two basic steps in the process. The first is the Design Phase

> **TIP:** Purchase an accordion-style file folder that will hold multiple files. Label your main sections such as Architecture, Construction, Contracts/ Invoices, Permits, Interior Design ....the list can go on and on and will grow as the project evolves, but start with these.

and the second is the Construction Phase. We will briefly cover each of them and what those steps entail but first you need to know where to start and what to do to keep everything in order.

As you gather information, you will need a way to keep it organized so that you can find documents when you need them.   Keep all these important documents together so you can easily reference what is needed and what information you have for each stage of your project. Keep a copy of all your invoices and contracts, so, if needed, you can go back to them as a reference.

Another great idea is to set up a spreadsheet with this information. Do not rely on others to keep track of all of this – <u>do it yourself</u>.

Design

When I speak of "design," I'm referring to combining all of the items that you want or need to incorporate into your project and turning them into real spaces by laying it all out on paper. This is the fun part! Proper planning and design leads to a successful project. We may have great visions in our heads, but if we can't explain to others what we would like, the design is just a dream with nothing to back it up. **Remember: A picture is worth a thousand words!**

The first item to consider with the design stage: what are you permitted to do within the constraints of your local zoning laws and regulations? Are there height restrictions in your town or setbacks from property lines that will limit your project? If you're looking to build a new home, are there

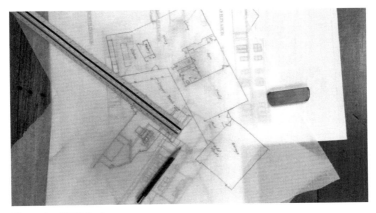

Photo by PDRdesigns

limits (such as environmental issues) to where on the property you can build? All of these questions should be answered in the planning stage of your project. The best resource for answers is a local architect; based on their experience, they will be aware of the specific site requirements that various towns in your area impose.

At the beginning of design, would also be the time to incorporate an Interior Designer.

> **TIP:** Pinterest, Houzz, and Google Images are great places to find examples of houses and details that you might like. Print them out, put them in your files, and review them with your architect so they can get a feel for the type of house and level of detail that you are expecting.

Christine Tuttle, Interior Designer and Owner of Christine Tuttle Design believes in involving an Interior Designer early on in the process so you can correctly budget them into the project. Collaboration with the Interior Designer, Architect, Builder, and Owner is key at this stage and allows the Interior Designer to give guidance along the way. This is a luxury service and owners hire an Interior Designer when they want a specific look or feel to their home. Interior Designers are able to take all of the different ideas you have and create a theme throughout the home. Put simply, they make your home special!

Photo by Keller + Keller

Christine Tuttle Design
PO Box 1355, Dedham, MA 02027
Phone: 508-737-0136
Email: *Christine@christinetuttle.com*
Website: *www.christinetuttle.com*

Construction

Speak to your homeowners' insurance company to understand what additional insurance you may need to provide during the project. Typically, a Builders' Risk policy is needed to protect the home during construction, so be sure to understand what you need to do to maintain adequate coverage. This is very important as many people don't properly prepare themselves with insurance coverage until it's too late. Understand what contractors' insurance covers and know where your insurance will need to fill in the gaps.

During the design process, you should be looking for a General Contractor. Your architect will be able to give you recommendations and referrals. The construction is the most complex and exciting part of the journey, where you finally get to watch as your vision materializes. The General Contractor is a major piece to this puzzle and you must be comfortable and have trust in him to build a quality project within your budget. Keep track of all contracts, invoices, material selections, change orders, bills paid, permits received, inspections, etc. during the process so that you can easily reference the documents you need. Keeping your files organized will give you peace of mind during this sometimes hectic process.

Following these basic planning and organizing steps will get you started on this journey to a fun and successful project! **Enjoy the trip, keep the destination in mind, and take lots of pictures along the way!**

When your project is complete, don't forget to put all of your Appliance Manuals, Warranties and Operating Instructions in a neatly labeled binder. Keep a file with all the names of contractors you may need to call in case of emergency for security systems, plumbing, electric, etc.

TIP: Have a calendar that lists the year and months where you can keep track of items such as: when filters need to be changed, batteries checked, fireplace chimneys cleaned and whatever other preventative maintenance is required. This can be reviewed once a month to see what items may need to be addressed and gives you peace of mind that all systems are running smoothly.

Photo by PDRdesigns   Before

This waterfront home undertook an addition and full makeover by PDRdesigns. The Jersey Shore theme is carried through every room.

Photo by PDRdesigns   After

3 BUDGET

The project budget is probably the biggest item that gives people anxiety – and rightfully so! I have worked with clients who have large budgets and those who have small budgets. One of the similarities I've found is that each client wants to maximize their dollars spent for a *return on investment* – which of course makes sense! The part that doesn't make sense, though, is the decisions that are made at times by clients during the process.

> *"Got no checkbooks, got no banks. Still I'd like to express my thanks - I've got the sun in the mornin' and the moon at night."*
>
> — *Irving Berlin*

One of the most important questions I ask my clients has to do with their total budget. The budget will determine the way the house is designed and built. Put simply, the budget equates to how much time is spent on a project. A simple addition or a house with a reasonable budget will take a set amount of time and is easy to figure for pricing – but a more elaborate house with a large budget is more complicated. There are many variables that can take significant amounts of time to design and build. When you tell your architect and builder what your budget is, it should be the actual budget. Be sure to communicate whether it's a firm number or a ballpark. You should always include 10%-15% for "extra" items and adjustments that need to be accounted for as the project progresses.

The budget is the driving force of the project because the expectations of each client are very different. Personally, I love both the jobs with a modest budget where the owner wants something well-built that doesn't require a lot of maintenance, as well as the elaborate jobs with exotic materials and lots of detail. However, you need to keep in mind that these are two very different situations and the owners' expectations for time spent coordinating and making selections for each are **very** different – and so they must be treated and priced

that way. A $15 door knob and a $500 door knob require vastly different levels of care, precision, and specifications.

I often say that a picture is worth a thousand words, and I will repeat it here regarding budget. Pictures of structures/ details that are close to what you want will go a long way towards conveying exactly what you are expecting. Additionally, this will ensure that you really understand what your budget will get you. There are builders that will build for $100 per square foot (PSF) and ones that build for $500 per square foot. And I assure you that you *will* get what you pay for – if you really think that you can get a larger, better house from the $100 PSF contractor than you can from the $500 PSF contractor… well, I would strongly advise you to lower your expectations! If you are basing the size of house or addition on a square foot cost, make sure that you include the basement, garage, porches and decks. Many people think the square foot cost only applies to living space, but obviously it costs something to build these items, so they must be factored in somewhere.

Pricing is based on the level of craftsmanship and care that goes into the project, and you will get completely different levels of service and vastly different results from different contractors. Whether it's what you want to hear or not, ultimately, that is the bottom line. The "more affordable" painter will not cover finishes carefully, or protect knobs and glass, or prepare the surface properly by

Custom Details, PDRdesigns

sanding and cleaning prior to painting. This all goes back, once again, to knowing what your budget will get you so you have a reasonable understanding and
expectation of the level of care and precision going into your project.

> **TIP:** At the end of the book, I have included a form for breaking out
> different line items in a project; I also provided a rough breakdown
> of percentages for each item. This is provided as a reference to give
> you an idea of the main categories that must be included. This is not a
> comprehensive list, but it is a very good start to help you understand
> the scope of work involved. I recommend that you review it and think
> about the different categories. You do not need to fill this in (you may
> not even know most items), but it will help you engage in a meaningful
> dialogue with your builder and architect.

Keeping track of your budget should be a fairly simple and straightforward task. I recommend creating a filing system broken down into the various project categories. Once you have your system set up, fill in items and file papers by these categories so you have all the information readily available whenever you need it!

The most important item to establish is how much you would like to spend and then understand what is possible for that amount of money.

Some people may be hesitant to set a budget as they are not sure what items cost; however, whether you are building a small addition or a new 10,000-square foot custom home, everyone needs to know what they are comfortable spending. This does not need to be an exact number, but having an idea of what you would like to spend on the project will help guide decisions as you progress.

The budget will also help you set realistic goals. I have had clients approach me wanting to build a small addition with an excessively large budget; on the other hand, I have had clients that dreamt of a large addition with an unreasonably low budget. Many times clients just don't understand costs and have no idea what the project will cost. In asking local builders or architects about costs, it will help you with your planning. There is no sense in wasting time planning an entire second floor addition with a $15,000 budget. On the other hand, I have clients who say they are planning to spend $2,000,000 but it is not a hard number and getting their wish list is more important than the total cost.

It is important for you to know what you can spend and then understand roughly what that amount of money will allow you to build. Of course the quality of construction is where the amounts vary greatly. Don't ever assume that you are getting the same product when someone quotes you half the price of the other guy.

For those of you that have no idea where to start or what you should expect a project to cost, I recommend discussing this with your architect to get a better understanding before establishing your budget. Budget is at the beginning of this book, since it is a major component of the design and construction of your project. Having a firm grasp of this item will help immensely with all of the following sections.

Even if you are only talking about rough budgets, understand what is included in those prices. Site work and landscaping is often an additional cost and interior items such as cabinetry and appliances may be as well. There are always unknown costs so be sure to understand what will not be done, as much as you understand what will be done. All for these items need to be added into your final project costs.

Photo by PDRdesigns   Before

Nestled in the woods, this family needed room to Grow! PDRdesigns completed a full renovation and addition to accommodate all their needs.

Photo by PDRdesigns   After

4 ARCHITECT OR CONTRACTOR FIRST?

A football team uses a quarterback to execute plays and keep all of the members of the team organized. Within the context of a home improvement project, this is the role of the architect as well. By starting with an architect, you will get critical project planning information that will allow you to see the full scope of the project. You must understand what can and cannot be done on your site prior to involving a contractor and obtaining pricing.

> *Faith is taking the first step, even when you don't see the whole staircase.*
>
> *— Martin Luther King Jr*

If you know you want to use the service of a specific contractor, that's great! Contact them, discuss the general idea of your project, then ask them to provide a recommendation of an architect with whom they work. (**See the chapter on "Hiring an Architect" for more information on this part of the process.**)

As mentioned before, often one of the biggest obstacles owners encounter is keeping their project within their budget. Some contractors will argue that if you start with an architect, you will end up with a design that exceeds your budget; on the other hand, most architects will argue that by starting

Photo by PDRdesigns   Grand Custom Stairway

with a contractor, you will end up with a drawing of a box without any detail! I have personally witnessed both situations, and I can tell you that neither "rule" is accurate – except in cases where *communication* broke down.

When you, the owner, bring in a contractor first, it is up to you to clearly communicate what you would like the end result to be and what you are willing to spend. It is also up to you to read how well the contractor listens and feeds this information back to you. Do not rely on words alone. Look at their past work. Notice how they react to your budget and your expectations. Show them pictures of what you'd like, and gauge how well they understand what you're saying.

However, the same holds true if you bring in an architect first. You must communicate clearly and pay close attention to the way the architect relays information back to you. Again, have them look at pictures of what you expect and take notice of their response. Review their past projects. If your budget isn't flexible, find out how they plan to keep costs in check. Most architects can recommend contractors they work with. When going this route, you should still get a contractor involved early in the process so you can make sure your professionals are onboard and working to make your dreams a reality within your budgetary constraints. This is your team of professionals.

As an architect, my recommendation is – of course – to hire an architect first.

Don't allow a builder to design your project as their focus tends to be budget driven rather than what's the best design and function for you and your family.

In my experience, the most successful projects are the ones that start with the architect and builder. Together, they create the team of other professionals, from surveyors and engineers to interior designers and landscape architects. Everyone has a role and the design should be well thought out with all of your wants and needs addressed up front. Having your entire team (including your interior designer) set early in the process allows everyone to work together to create the dream home that you want.

Marlaina Teich, Interior Designer, joined me to talk about when to incorporate an Interior Designer.

For best results with an Interior Designer, Marlaina suggests involving an Interior Designer early in the design process. This way they can help with flooring colors, styles and selections, cabinets, and countertops, trim, hardware and lighting fixtures and layouts. When all these are selected with a whole project design and feel, then the paint colors, window treatments and furniture can pull it all together. Having this cohesive idea from the start is how an Interior Designer turns this empty space into your home!

If you are looking for a single room design, you should budget about $1,500- $2,500 per room. This will include selections for paint colors, fabrics and furniture.

For a new home, you should budget about $5per SF for beginning to end interior design. Hiring an Interior Designer gives you the peace of mind that all you selections will integrate beautifully in your new home!

Marlaina Teich Design
2605 Merrick Rd. Bellmore, NY 11710
Phone: 516-378-0228
Email: *marlaina@mtdny.com*
Website: *www.mtdny.com*

Photo by Ric Marder Photography   Interior Designer – Marlaina Teich

5 HIRING AN ARCHITECT

The single biggest problem in communication
is the illusion it has taken place.

— George Bernard Shaw

Architects spend years in rigorous schoolings, working as interns, and then passing a 9 part exam to be licensed. They understand proportions and zoning and building codes and are able to communicate what you would like built, through the use of pictures and drawings. This is a unique gift and makes the process of utilizing a licensed architect rewarding and fun! Be open to new ideas and different options along the way as they may see possibilities that you did not consider. Ask about timeframes upfront so you know what to expect and roughly how long the various stages will take.

Photo by PDRdesigns

This portion of the process is both design and personality based. You need an architect that will, first and foremost, listen to you and your needs and wants, and translate that into a structure specifically designed for you. With that being said, I would like to stress the importance of communication between yourself and your architect. Be specific as to what you want your project to look like. This will give the architect the ability to design a project that is as close to what you are looking for as possible.

The number one complaint I hear about architects is that they don't listen, and when the owner views the proposed design, they find it's not even close to what they wanted. This disconnect may also be related to what was communicated to the architect, so be as specific and clear as you can.

When hiring an architect, keep in mind that you are the one in control. They are the expert, but you are hiring them to do a job, and they work for you. Don't feel anxious or intimidated to ask what you might think are

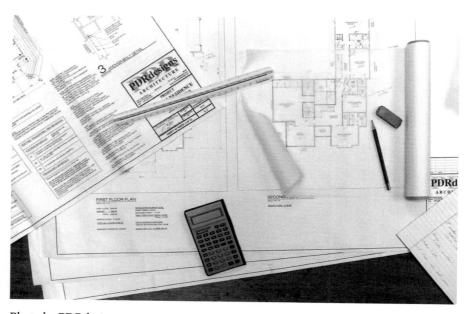

Photo by PDRdesigns

"silly" questions. If you don't understand something, speak up – they will be happy to inform and educate you until you do understand.

It's a smart idea to have questions prepared when you start making calls to screen potential architects. Because the relationship you have with your professionals is important, you should make sure you feel comfortable with them and have a good rapport in order to establish good communication. Start with this list:

- What is your mission statement?
- Have you designed similar projects and can I see pictures of them?
- Who in your firm will I be dealing with and what experience do they have?
- What sets your firm apart from other firms in the area?
- How does the process unfold from design through construction?
- What am I expected to provide during the design process?
- Will I have opportunities to alter the design as we progress?
- How will you present the project to me? Plans and elevations, 3-D renderings, models?
- How does your firm bill for services rendered?

When you find a few architects you like over the phone, make appointments to meet them in person. Think of it as a job interview where you are the employer – because that's exactly what you are. Sit down with them and describe briefly the scope of the project that you would like them to design. For example, you might say: "We want to expand the kitchen and great room about 12' by removing the back wall of the house. On the second floor, we'd like to add a bedroom and expand the master bath. The backyard will have a new deck, about 12'x24'. We'd like a pergola on the right for shade, and a grilling/bar area on the left." Have pictures of similar projects that you like on hand to help describe your wants and needs. When you're clear about what you would like in a quick overview, it's much easier for the architect to grasp the project. The next step is to then ask if they've done similar projects, and if so, to provide pictures and references so you can follow up.

Once you have completed your meeting process and checked references, you should ask for a proposal for the design work for your project. Read through the proposal carefully, making sure that the scope of work written matches your understanding of what they will provide. If you have questions, make a list so that you can be sure to address all of your concerns. Make sure that the fees are spelled out clearly and that you understand what is included in the fee and what is not included.

The general steps that are covered with Architectural Services are:

Stage 1: Documenting Existing Conditions – measuring all existing buildings, floor plans and elevations in order to establish a beginning point for all renovations and addition projects.

Stage 2: Discovery and Programming

Discovery – Evaluating the current building site including zoning and code research.

Programming – Identifying the homeowner's needs and wants and together establishing a clear scope of the work to be completed.

Stage 3: Schematic Design – Rough sketches are created to provide the client a beginning point for discussion. This stage is about traffic flow through the house and site and functional relationships. Since design is a fluid process, nothing is hard lined at this point. It may take 1 or 2 more iterations before the Client approves the schematic design and moves to the next phase.

Stage 4: Design Development - Refining the rough sketches into plans, elevations and detailed drawings. Materials and mechanical systems will be discussed during this stage. These drawings will form the basis for the construction documents and will be approved by the owner before moving forward. This is the time we like to identify consultants to include on the project team. The best projects are the result of the combined efforts of the Client, Architect, Designers, and Contractors.

Stage 5: Construction Documents – Providing detailed documents so the permits can be obtained. All jurisdictions require a code compliant set of documents to issue a building permit. These are the drawings that contain all of the notes, details, and diagrams for the Building Department to issue construction permits and the contractors to provide final pricing.

Additional Services that Architects can offer are:

1. Bidding and negotiation, where your architect will help you choose a contractor and review the construction bids to compare and contrast the proposals from General Contractors.

2. Construction Administration through which your architect will function as your agent, verifying the contractor is following the plans, helping with any questions that arise during the construction process and review billings and the schedule. Your architect is not "supervising" the project but checking for plan conformity.

3. Interior Design details – if those were not completed during the process of the original architectural services and you are not hiring an interior designer then the Architect is often brought in to select trim styles and layout, provide cabinetry designs or fireplace mantels or any other special features that may be added along the way.

Find an architect that you get along with and feels like a good fit. They are an integral part of your project and will help to make your building adventure a memorable one!

This waterfront home replaced one damaged by Hurricane Sandy. Designed by PDRdesigns and built by Discola Contracting, this home is the essence of the Jersey Shore Beach Style. These images show the progression from concept sketch to rendering to construction and final completion.

6 SITE - ENGINEERING AND SELECTION

Any fool can Know, The point is to understand.
— Albert Einstein

Understanding your site, the particular constraints that come with it and what you can do on that site is critical to the success of your project. What you will be allowed to do with your site will depend on where it is located.

The 3 most important items to look for are: **location, location, location**. This is the old adage, but it still holds true! You must understand your property and the surrounding area. Are there busy roads nearby, train tracks, a commercial building? Drive the area to be sure you understand where shopping centers are nearby, how close you are to any items you may consider negative and what the property looks like in winter without any trees and leaves covering a view. Pull up google satellite images of the site to be able to see the surrounding area from above. For a truly amazing background of your property, buy a detailed report on MyFloodStatus.com that will show aerial views through the years, give you locations of nearby waterways or farmland preservation areas and tell you if there are

PROPERTY PEEK REPORT
Wetlands
Elevation: 6,000 feet (scale: 1" = 500 feet)

NJ PROPERTY FAX

Photo by myfloodstatus.com
This is an example of a wetlands map prorided as a part of the total report provided by myfloodstatus.com

environmental constraints. I met Patti and Rob, owners of Western Technologies Group (WTG), the parent company of MyFloodStatus.com and immediately knew they had a great product. I recommend this small (less than $50) investment as it gives you so much information!

After you understand the surrounding area, you will need to know where your building can be located on your site. This information will be a combination of an Engineer, Architect, or the town Zoning Department. If you want to get information on your own, a trip to the town zoning department may give you the answers you need. They should be able to tell you the site size and what the setbacks are for the front, sides and back and provide you with a chart showing all of this information.

Other information that you may find useful are what are the schools like in the area, are there any deed restrictions or easements on the property (your survey from your engineer will show this), do you have a Home Owners Association (HOA) that will regulate what you can or cannot do to your house, does the house have well or city water, is there a sewer line to the street or a septic system? By the way if you have a septic system, the design of the septic systems is based on the number of bedrooms only, so if you are planning to add a bedroom, your septic system may need to be updated and Heath Department Approval needed before filing construction permits with the town.

Understanding your site constraints is a major piece of the puzzle, so be sure to do your due diligence before undertaking the project! Seek professional advice and have your Architect coordinate this process, so the entire team understands your particular site and works collectively toward your goals!

TIP: For a more detailed understanding of your exact site, hire a local surveyor to layout your survey, do a topographic survey and a soil boring so that you know what type of soil you are built on and how deep the ground water is. They can also layout the zoning setbacks on the survey so you can easily see where you can add to your existing house or build new.

7 DESIGN

"Less is More" - Ludwig Mies van der Rohe

Now comes the *fun* part – letting your creativity loose! We've already touched on why hiring an architect to create your vision is well worth the investment. **An architect's role in the project is problem-solving – this is where we excel!**

Personally I love this part of the project because we, the architects, get to basically act like kids again. We sketch, we draw, we can be messy and just enjoy the thrill of creating something amazing! There are no "right" or "wrong" answers in design work – go ahead and explore crazy options and whimsical ideas that you like. Eventually, you'll find yourself naturally narrowing down the things you love and want from the things you merely like; but at this stage I encourage you to think as abstractly and "different" as you like so that all avenues are explored.

Although thinking outside the box is encouraged, you must still clearly communicate with your architect. Without clear communication, two people can be discussing the same project and still be visualizing vastly different designs. The best way to avoid that is to use pictures and sketches to express your thoughts. I discovered this truth early in my career when talking to clients and contractors.

The client, contractor, and I were discussing a trim detail for an archway into a great room. The contractor would describe how he was planning to handle it and then the owner would describe what he wanted. I quickly realized they were each thinking of totally different approaches, even though what they were saying was similar. I proceeded to draw a picture of what I thought the owner wanted to see, with some creative possibilities to what could be done. The owner liked it and the contractor now fully understood what was expected of him. Without this simple picture, the owner would have been disappointed in what was built, while the contractor would not understand the frustration. Pictures, simple as they may be, save time and understanding in any situation ... a picture is truly worth a thousand words or shall we say dollars. Reworking a sketch is much less expensive than rebuilding something you don't like. You do not need to be Michelangelo to be able to express your ideas. A simple sketch will almost always work.

Photo by PDRdesigns   Architectural Ceiling Design and Archway
Architect-PDR designs
Trim by W.F.Sherman and son Millwork, Manasquan, NJ Interior Design by Suzette Donleavy General contractor -James Lukowitz

There are a few simple steps I recommend to start your design process. First, get a binder to save all of your ideas. If you prefer a more "modern" approach, also create an online Ideabook on Houzz or a board on Pinterest. Feel free to add pictures and designs that express your style. Remember this is supposed to be fun – so enjoy yourself! If your project has exterior as well as interior elements then break out the binder into the relevant sections – for example: Site Design, Exterior, and Interior. Each of these sections can then be broken down into the needed parts.

Here are some suggestions:
Site Design: Driveway, Landscaping, Lighting, Paths, Pool, Pergola, Fence.
Exterior: Roofing, Siding, Windows, Trim Details, Porch, Lights.
Interior: Kitchen, Great Room, Living Room, Dining Room, Master Suite, Bedroom 2, Bedroom 3, Shared Bathroom, Laundry Room

These sections can be adapted as needed for your project by adding or removing the relevant parts.

The next step is to begin to collect images of what it is that you like for each of these spaces or items. In order to be clear with your thoughts, mark up the pictures as you put them into your binder so that you remember

> **TIP:** Use magazines, books, online searches, and pictures to assemble a collection of ideas that you would like to incorporate into your design.

exactly what it is you like about the item. If it is a picture of a house and you like the window shown, then circle it and write: Trim Style, Size, Color, or Grille Pattern, to explain what it is particularly that you like about the image. Don't feel pressured here as you are not yet designing your space; this is just to express your likes and dislikes so that others understand what it is that you would like to see. When you are ready to talk to an architect, show them your scrapbook so that they will have a much better understanding of the styles and details that are pleasing to you. However, it's important to remember that this chapter started with the quote "**Less is more**" for a reason. Simply put, if you have sixteen different window styles circled, then you will not be clarifying – you will be confusing! Sure, you can select a couple of different pictures, but do not overwhelm someone with vastly different styles. It is also important for all people involved in the design process to agree on what they like. For example, I was working with a couple and the husband liked a Modern Style, while the wife preferred a more Beach Style house. This style difference created challenges as we went around and around with design until I was able to negotiate with them which parts were most important to each and then incorporated their style into the design elements that they felt were most fitting. When a couple cannot agree on what they like, then it is very difficult for an architect to create a design that both people will like. Have these discussions up front with each other and your architect to allow for a smoother design process.

This process can be repeated with each of the sections you have created and you can add as much or as little detail to your design as you wish. Work on creating the overall spaces first and then concentrate on the details for those spaces. Create your binder at your leisure, whether that is over a period of days or months as you are thinking about and planning your project. Many owners start thinking about an idea well before they actually start to do something about it, so use that time to clarify and simplify your thoughts and desires. If there are certain products that you would like to

use in your project, you can create a section for those as well and then you will not forget to discuss them with your architect and builder.

Again, don't feel pressure to get all of these pictures and ideas together. This is supposed to be the fun and enjoyable part! If you like, sit down with your spouse or your kids and let it be a fun, free, collaborative evening of creativity and dreaming. Do what feels right to you – let the ideas flow. If you find that you're *not* enjoying this part, it's perfectly fine to step back and let your architect do the design work. I will tell you that the more involved and emotionally connected you are to a project, the more rewarding and exciting the design process will be.

> *"Nothing Great was ever achieved without Enthusiasm"*
>
> — *Emerson*

Now that we have a game plan set up as to *how* we can work on the designs, I will give you a room-by-room breakout of the major design items to consider in each of the main spaces. Here we go ...

Front Entry

I like to begin thinking about the design of a house with the front entry. What feelings do you want it to evoke? I'm not talking about the site, or landscaping, or pathways – but when you look at the front of the house, what do you want it to say? Entries can be subtle, extravagant, inviting, bold, comfortable, or even intimidating. It all depends on how you want to welcome your guests – but more importantly, how do you want to feel when you arrive home each night?

Photo by PDRdesigns

I was recently working on a renovation of a home and the approach and front entry were a major concern. Debra, my client, wanted a grander entry, something that stood out and announced you had arrived. Her teenage daughter was more concerned with feeling protected. We ultimately decided to go with a low wall with a wrought iron gate vestibule directly outside the front door. To make the entry more defined, we created a front courtyard and limestone columns supporting wooden timber trusses. This provided the wow factor, safety and a covering at the front door, satisfying everyone's concerns.

A covered entry is essential to protect you and the front door from the weather.

This can be as simple as a small covered porch or it could be a large deck across the front of the house! Consider what type of door you'd like as well. Would solid wood give you a treasured feeling of protection, or would you prefer glass, which is more welcoming? Or maybe you'd like a combination of the two!

Photo by PDRdesigns
Custom front door on a waterfront home.

Suzette Donleavy, Interior Designer and Owner of Well Designed Interiors talks about Front Entries and the importance of good design in an excerpt below.

"Once the architect has incorporated the details for the Front Entry, it is equally important to plan the space beyond the front door starting with the foyer. Your foyer should excite your guest as to what lies in the rooms ahead. A fabulous chandelier sets the stage! Can you compliment the lighting with sconces that could frame artwork? The architectural details in your home begin here as well...crown moulding, wainscot or do you have the luxury of a timeless fully-paneled space? Do you have the opportunity to create detail in the floor material? A herringbone pattern with the wood material, an inlayed medallion, or a timeless tile design with a border. Perhaps it is a statement wallpaper that sets the tone. And don't forget the furnishings, area rug, art and accessories to compliment the architectural foundation that has been designed. I also love to include seating...a chair that makes a statement or a painted bench accentuated with beautiful pillows bids your guest welcome. And don't forget a mirror for a quick check before you answer the door!"

"In the project Paul referenced with our client Debra, I had the unique opportunity to "flip" a gas fireplace from the adjoining living room that was in an awkward location in the room but was a spectacular feature in the foyer. I paired it with the family's baby grand piano. How elegant!"

Photo by Suzette Donleavy

Well Designed Interiors
119 East River Rd. Rumson, NJ 07760
Phone: 732-758-9090
Email: *suzette@welldesignedinteriors.com*
Website: *www.welldesignedinteriors.com*

When you step inside, what do you want to see and how do you want to feel? Do you want open views to the great room and kitchen? Is this a two-story entry? Is there a staircase leading your eyes upward? Consider what rooms you want on either side – and don't forget a coat closet!

Special items can be added for an additional "wow" factor, such as tile floor patterns and inlays, decorative columns, and trim to define the sense of arrival. What about ceiling details or light fixtures? Decorative ceilings grab your attention!

I worked on a house design where the client, Larry, had been to the Four Seasons Hotel in Boston and loved the railing detail on the steps. We recreated that railing on a sweeping staircase in the entry. Now, every time Larry walks upstairs, he has an emotional association with luxury and relaxation.

How we feel is what really transforms a house into a home!

Kitchen

> *"Good food and a warm kitchen is what makes a house a home"*
> — *Rachael Ray*

This is my favorite space to design. The kitchen says so much about its occupants' personality and style! When I think of a kitchen, I, like most people, associate it with growing up – whether it was with my parents, my grandmother, etc. I loved cooking with my mom and cooking is a lot like architecture… only *better!* I get to design buildings or houses, and then watch as they are built. When cooking, you get to create a meal or a dish and then not only see the results – but eat it, too!

My grandmother's kitchen was a special place. She was always baking pies or cookies, and as soon as I entered her house, I would be transfixed by the warm aromas. Even now, whenever I smell cookies baking, I drift back to those fond days as a child. To me, that's the essence of a kitchen. It is a gathering place – comfortable and functional, with ample space to sit and places to cook.

Most kitchens now have become larger and often include an island or peninsula with stools, as well as a table for everyday meals. The latest trend is eliminating the dining room altogether and using the space instead

Photo by Marco Ricco Photography
Designed by Marlaina Teich

for a larger kitchen that can work for all occasions. Exact cabinetry, styles, counters, colors, etc. will be determined with your kitchen cabinet shop or interior designer – but the basic cabinet and appliance layout will be shown on the architectural plans.

Consider what views you want from the kitchen. Generally you want a clear view of the yard to be able to keep an eye on any little ones playing, or depending on your location, you might want a view of the water or hillside. Most likely, the kitchen will be open to the great room or family room, and also the dining room. Consider whether you want doors to open the kitchen up to an exterior space, or if you just want access to the yard. Do you want a lot of pantry space? Perhaps a butler's pantry will meet your needs – this creates a space to keep some of the clutter out of the main kitchen and give you lots of extra storage. Some clients like to add an extra oven, refrigerator, and sink in this room. Essentially, it gives you a little extra freedom to build to suit your needs, as this space can either be simple or more involved.

Ceiling designs add a lot of character to a kitchen, but they must be planned properly in conjunction with the lighting layout. There is no right

Photo by Cara Realty
Architecture by PDRdesigns

or wrong ceiling design, though, so be creative here and add some dropped details or trim to spice it up a bit!

Other items to consider: What is the connection to the garage or mud-room? Often these spaces are off the kitchen, so be aware of how they will tie together; you don't want the workflow of the kitchen interrupted by people entering and exiting the garage. If you have children, this is also important for safety reasons with ovens and stoves.

Some key elements that also get overlooked in the kitchen: Do you want a TV in the kitchen? Personally I dislike this idea as I feel it is a room naturally oriented to family time, but some like to have this option. Would you like a sound system or speakers installed in the ceiling or walls, with wall pad controls or controls from your phone or tablet? Also, a pot filler at the stove is an item many clients desire as it helps them avoid carrying a full pot of water from the sink to the stove (although you will still need to carry it to the sink after it has cooked).

Photo & Architecture by PDRdesigns

Appliance options are too numerous to mention, so suffice it to say that you need to do your research! Understand all of the options and pricing before selecting appliances. Your cabinet shop or interior designer will also be able to help with these selections.

There may not be much wall space left after all of the cabinets, back-splashes, windows, and doors. A complementary paint color may work, or you might want to add a bit of texture with a Venetian-style plaster or a wood wainscotting.

Consider all of these separate items for the kitchen and think about them together to make sure the different elements all complement one another. Create the style that is unique to *you*. This room is a gathering space and you will be spending a lot of time there, so let it speak to your soul, inviting you in each morning.

"Vive bene, ama molto, ridi spesso"
"Live well, laugh often, love much"

Kristie Loughman, Tile Designer from Monmouth Street Tile talks about kitchen backsplashes.

Photo by Monmouth St. Tile   Photo by PDRdesigns

The kitchen backsplash can be a simple design to fade into the background or become an elegant focal point of the kitchen. One of the best places to add accent with tile is behind the cooktop. Add a color to the border, use a mosaic tile with a different texture or a hand painted tile to create the perfect feel of what your home and kitchen mean to you.

Keep in mind the locations of items such as pot fillers, outlets and switches and how they may impact your borders or special designs. If you plan correctly, there won't be any conflicts when installing.

Monmouth Street Tile
2175 Hwy 35 Sea Girt, NJ 08750
732 974-0048
44 Monmouth St.
Red Bank, NJ 07701
Phone: 732-933-1760
Website: *www.monmouthsttile.com*

Photo by PDRdesigns

Great Room

The "great room" is such an amazing name! Who wouldn't want to be in a room like that?

As implied, this should be a room that welcomes, inspires, and comforts you – a gathering space where friends and family are drawn and feel at home. So how do we create this evocative room?

I like to begin by deciding what location on the site will invite the best views. Perhaps you have an ocean or river view, or a pool or yard you'd like to see. Sometimes it might simply be avoiding the view you don't want to see! Now, think about which rooms you want adjacent to this space. The most popular layout is open to the kitchen, the other common gathering space for family and friends. This connection makes sense and allows for a smooth flow, both of people and of conversations.

How can you create the great room that you love? One of the most unifying and comforting ornamentations is a fireplace. This can be wood-burning for the hearty, adventurous type, or gas-burning when that is less work and a simple flip of the switch if desired. The fireplace serves as an anchor in the room, and with the right design, can be warm and inviting.

The views into the yard need to be considered – specifically, how you want to frame those views. What style window and/or doors, and what size and layout would work best? Basically, how much glass and what shape will make a huge difference in the feel of the space, and will also dictate how much the outdoors becomes an extension of the room. Other design items that can be considered are ceiling designs, such as a simple crown molding, applied trim, or wood beams – these can draw the eye upward and add that "wow" factor.

Cabinetry and shelving is another option that adds style to your space. I advise selecting books, family pictures, or even personal items you love such as model trains or travel souvenirs. Shelving and cabinetry can be as

Photo and Architecture by PDRdesigns

Wendi Smith, CEO and Founder of Leftover Luxuries, and an Interior Designer was kind enough to sit down with me to discuss decorating a Great Room like a World Class Interior Designer.

"Lighting is the most important element. Plan that early in the project, utilizing recessed lights, dimmer switches, and a hanging fixture. I used oversized hanging fixtures to make a statement as soon as you walk in the room. Ambient light from table lamps is essential to the feel of the space, too, so don't forget those floor plugs.

The Great Room is a gathering place which has to be warm, cozy and comfy. Whether you have 1 or 2 seating areas, always have throw rugs, pillows, and blankets to create that feel and to absorb sound. My favorite room designs have a mix of materials, stone, glass, leather and tufted ottomans with lots of texture! To complete that cozy feeling is one of my signature candle sconces.

A fireplace should have a mirror above it to reflect light, not a T.V., unless it's concealed, and the mantel and surround need to reflect the style of the room. A modern room will have a sleek surround while my traditional designs contain chunkier wood or stone surrounds.

The pieces that I choose to accessorize with are eclectic, but tie everything together. No matching end tables and lamps please. Pieces need to be collected over time and each has their own story behind them. Color variations and textural variety keep the space interesting.

So, how do I make this eclectic look all come together for a unified theme? It all hinges on color, texture, art, lighting and hiring a fabulous interior designer!

Photo by Wendi Smith

Wendi Smith, CEO & Founder of Leftover Luxuries
Interior Designer
www.leftoverluxuries.com
(434)989-3543
350 Pantops Center
Charlottesville, VA 22911

simple or ornate as you choose; it's up to your taste and the feeling you want to create. Whatever you choose, make sure it is *you*. This is your house – your personal space – so let it be an extension of your personality! That's the only way you will truly enjoy it.

Flooring for the great room presents another opportunity to do something different. Whether you like wood and want a simple border with another color, or pattern, or possibly tile designed to look like wood, make sure it complements the style you are creating and welcomes you to the space. Throw rugs are a great way to add charm and fresh texture to your room too.

Family Room

While the great room is a larger gathering space with sweeping views of the countryside (okay – maybe not *all* great rooms have that…) the family room is generally a smaller space off to the side of the main rooms. This is a comfortable TV room for relaxing. Often this space is overtaken by children and their toys to become a play room, but essentially it is a more relaxed, less formal room where you can put your feet up and be yourself.

Similar to the great room, a fireplace works well in this room as nothing says warmth and comfort like a hearth and a crackling fireplace. (Yes, this clearly comes from someone who endures freezing winters in

Photo and Architecture by PDRdesigns

New Jersey and loves chopping wood to relax and unwind!) The word "hearth" or heart was originally used to describe the fireplace. This was where cooking, warmth, and conversation all converged – truly the heart of the home. It is only fitting to have a hearth and fireplace in the family room.

Views to the yard and possible access in and out will play a role in the design of this room. You can make this as informal as you would like, but be sure that it is comfortable and enjoyable.

Design ideas – cabinetry to put away games and toys, wainscoting or wall trim to break up the wall surface, ceiling details, an accent wall where the fireplace/TV/both are located.

Living Room

With the great room becoming more common, the living room seems to be a thing of the past for most new homes. Typically, the living room connotes a more formal space for gathering. Depending on how you'd like to use this space, which will often depend on its location, you might find it easier to incorporate it into your great room or family room.

The living room in a smaller house is typically the great room and family room combined. In this case, we often find a kitchen, living room, bedroom, and bathrooms. When you are working with a smaller area, try to minimize the interior walls to maximize the feeling of spaciousness. Keep in mind what walls may be needed for windows, a TV, and furniture placement.

When planning the living room, keep in mind that you still want this room near the kitchen or great room. You can decide whether there is a more formal or informal feel; always go with your style and taste, and don't feel you have to create anything based on others' input. **Let your heart do the talking here and design a space that just feels right for you!**

Dining Room

My childhood memories are of a dining room that was used a few times a year, when we would pack it full of family and bring extra tables and chairs to accommodate all of my relatives. Although we made great memories there – the smell of freshly baked pies, the warmth of the coffee brewing,

Photo and Architecture by PDRdesigns

and the giggling of children – the room wasn't often used and sometimes seemed like wasted space.

When I design now, I try to incorporate the dining room into the flow of the house – or, I do away with it altogether in favor of a larger eat-in kitchen. Many owners would rather have this layout with an island and a large table for dining, rather than a separate room that would not be used often. However, there are some owners that prefer the dining room and rather than use it only a few times a year, make it the space for everyday eating in lieu of an eat-in kitchen. Of course, we still have people that prefer the traditional dining room for occasional eating/use with extended family. Whatever your preference, there are certain items that must be considered for the design of the dining room.

Access to the kitchen is, naturally, critical – so keep this room open to and adjacent to the cooking area for an easy workflow of food, dishes, and people!

Views are great if this room can overlook some open space, but not essential as most of the focus would be on people and food. Lighting is typically a chandelier of some style and I recommend additional recessed lights for when a brighter view is needed. I know my dining room also doubles as a reading room, meeting space, party room, and office – thus adaptable lighting is essential.

Wainscoting and wide trims are a great look for this room and will set it apart from other spaces. Make the entry a bit wider, add decorative columns or wider trims up the sides and at the top of the openings to announce that this is a special place. This trim can be traditional, modern, or any other style – as always, the most important factor is that it reflects you.

Wall covering/wallpaper can be used on an accent wall above the wainscoting, or on all the walls to set this space apart. Ceiling trims, tin ceiling design, and crown moulding will dress this space up – and don't forget to use a different color paint for the ceiling! This can be a slightly different shade from the walls, or something totally different that will make the room stand out. Utilize pictures or decorative mirrors on the walls that complete the look and feel you're trying to convey.

Office

A home office is a room that is being incorporated into more houses these days as working from home and entrepreneurial endeavors become more and more common. This is a room that can be closed off from the rest of the house for the privacy needed to conduct business, and to keep little hands from using important documents as coloring books!

For a long time, I had my office on the third floor of my house, which gave me my own space and a (mostly!) quiet environment. Many clients prefer an office adjacent to the master bedroom or on the first floor, set away from the main gathering rooms. Wherever you elect to place yours, consider what you will need to have in it to get the sizing correct. The most common items are a desk, cabinetry with doors and bookshelves, and an additional chair or two. You can have built-in cabinetry designed or you can keep it as simple as shelving from Ikea.

A library may be a part of your office or for the bibliophile, may contain shelves full of books or a comfortable chair to read. Try to have some natural light in the room so that it feels welcoming and conducive to productivity.

Photo and Architecture by PDRdesigns

Photo by PDRdesigns
Custom Cabinetry by Sherman Millwork Cabinetry

If you have awards, diplomas, or certificates of achievements, display them proudly! They serve as great conversation starters when you have friends or clients over.

Master Suite

Many years after I built my house, my master bedroom was still not completed. The trim was put up quickly just to get it in and the walls were only partially painted. Finally, one day I was fed up of going to bed and waking up to see an unfinished room! I needed a place to relax, an escape, so I planned and finally completed my room. I added a small bar for morning coffee or a nightly glass of wine. I installed beadboard and trim on the ceiling, built a new mantel above my fireplace, added lighting, picked up a few new pieces of furniture, and repainted the walls and ceiling. What a difference it made – both for the room and my attitude! Now, every night, I see a calming, relaxing space before I go to sleep. When I wake, I look around and find myself thankful for my peaceful retreat and ready to start the day!

One of many owners' concerns is whether to put the master suite on the first floor (as many older couples prefer) or on the second floor with the other bedrooms. Generally, if you have young children, I would recommend having all of the bedrooms on the same floor. For a ranch house, that's the default option; for a two-story home, this would be a personal preference.

Consider where you will have views, where you will be facing away from traffic and/or neighbors, and what rooms you will be above when planning this room. Decide what amenities you want for your master suite retreat.

Consider a wet bar area, sitting room, balcony, fireplace, attached office space, separate walk-in closets, separate his-and-her baths, control panel for the house interior/exterior lights, and/or an alarm control panel. Some sort of ceiling detail should be added as you are often looking up while lying in bed.

Dana Nicholson, Interior Designer and Owner of Nicholson Studios in NYC, took time out of his busy day to sit down and talk with me about Master Bedroom Design. Dana has worked both nationally and internationally and has been published throughout his career for his exceptional Interior Design. His clients range from the average owner looking to rework a room, to high net worth clients looking to acquire a multi-million dollar painting.

Master Bedroom Suites were the focus of our conversation and his idea of the ideal Master Bedroom Suite. "The room has to be about your passions, places you've traveled to. It should be uplifting, different and contain memories, snippets of your life and unique items that resonate with you! For the walls, find artwork or pictures that express your soul. One of the greatest challenges an interior designer faces is getting to know a client's likes and dislikes, so they can choose pieces that sing to them. Don't get caught up trying to find frames and styles that all match, go with the eclectic look, but be sure that each piece has meaning and is personal. Items can be inexpensive or luxurious but the key is to have them represent your lifestyle. To make it unique, think outside the big box retailers and check out your local flea market, thrift store, and yard sale. I love saleing (traveling from yard sale to yard sale) and finding unique items that fit into my spaces. Make an adventure of it and take your time looking for those meaningful items that will create your look. There is no deadline, so enjoy the exploring and continue that emotional attachment. When it comes to the headboard, remember, it's the focal point of the room. It can be grand or understated but it centers the space and all its belongings so it should appeal to you.

Remember to do something special for this room that will relax you at night and allow you to wake up and start your day with a smile!

Photo by Dana Nicholson Studio   Photo by Dana Nicholson Studio

Dana Nicholson
Interior Designer
Owner, Dana Nicholson Studio, Inc.
438 West 37th St., New York, NY 10018, (212) 966-4000
www.Nicholsonstudio.com

Photo and Architecture by PDRdesigns

Master Bathroom

Part of the Master Suite is the Master Bathroom. There are so many options for bathrooms these days. What I have found to be consistent with clients is a large shower instead of a separate tub and shower. Sure there are still clients that would like a tub, but most people only want it because they feel it's needed for resale. If you will use it, then certainly have a tub, but don't design one in just because you feel that others will want it.

Another want list item is 2 separate vanities or at least a double vanity. Your vanity should include upper cabinets for your miscellaneous items you use every day. A linen closet is great if it fits in the space. Often times this is made of the same cabinetry as the vanity. The toilet should be separated by a half wall when possible or even a separate room entirely, which is currently popular. As this room is part of your relaxing Master Suite, do something special here. Spend a little more on the shower tile and shower fixtures. Add a few body sprays or a rain head shower head. Look at frameless glass doors, wall tiles options and towel bars that will accent the room. Simple ceiling designs or crown moulding can add that touch of luxury you want here.

Photo by Monetti Custom Homes

Photo by Monetti Custom Homes

Robert Jennings, Interior Designer and Owner of Robert Jennings Design took some time to explain to me the essential components for a stunning Master Bathroom Design.

Having a background in the fashion industry, I understand what looks good with a client. Design begins by understanding my client and their lifestyle, seeing the color palettes that will compliment them and utilizing that information mixed with a firm belief that form follows function.

To properly design a client's new space, I look at the way they live in their existing space- do they take lots of vitamins, medicines, or use many hair products that need to be stored? This determines the first elements: how much cabinet space is needed in a vanity with drawers, recessed medicine cabinet or full height linen closet. At times a Master Bathroom will work with a double vanity, and other times 2 separate vanities are required. Lighting is an element that is often overlooked, but is crucial to this room. There should be recessed lights on dimmers and directional light with wall sconces that light up your face. Like all rooms, this should be an experience and your wall treatments are essential. Subway tiles will give you a simple, clean look and can be run floor to ceiling or stopped halfway up the wall and capped with a border. Don't stop at chair rail height as this will feel too low in a bathroom. The classic "shore feel" can be accomplished with a wood or tile wainscot. This divides the walls top to bottom and the cap provides a shelf for shells or small frames with art work. To save money and still get an elegant look, create marble inlay on the floors or walls as an accent. Honeycombe tiles are my favorite floor treatment as they add visual interest and can be the entire floor or an inset. Use the same tiles in varying shapes and sizes so it doesn't get too busy and when designing a children's bath, don't be too juvenile with the tile as they will outgrow this quickly. Whimsical artwork is easier to swap out later.

Light colors and white makes a room appear larger and glass shower doors versus curtains have the same effect. Bring in color with towels and artwork. Mirrors with great lighting are essential for getting yourself ready.

What finishes should you use for fixtures? I love polished nickel, although it shows lots of fingerprints and chrome always maintains that shore feel and is timeless for any environment. The last item – shower storage. Create extra wall niches to avoid bottles all over your shower floors.

Keep with these basics and you will love your bathroom retreat!

Robert Jennings, Interior Designer
www.robertjenningsdesign.com
908-409-1860
New Hope, PA 18938

Photo by Robert Jennings

Master Closet

The most common joke my clients, ok wives, tell me is that she would like a large walk in closet and the husband can use a hook on the wall. (laughter... pause ...) In reality, the preference is two separate walk in closets, when possible, and yes the wives closet always seems to be a bit larger.

Closet designs range from simple wire style shelves to wood cubbies and shelving to elaborate cabinetry with glass doors and center islands. You don't need a huge space since there are so many ways to get lots of storage in small areas, but feel free to make this space special to you as you will use it every day.

Photo by californiaclosets.com

Bedrooms

The trend is for smaller, more efficient bedrooms with more detail. A full guest suite with an attached bath is popular for parents or children that may be moving back in or simply for overnight guests.

Bedrooms don't need to be huge to be effective. Important design ideas to consider are: a desk for homework, a window seat with a bench for storage below, shelving for books and pictures, a decorative special furniture piece or wall hanging to catch the eye, a throw rug, window placement, a door and balcony and simple ceiling design. Ceiling fans create a soothing breeze on those hot summer nights. Elegant or whimsical, these ideas will work for all settings. You don't need to incorporate all of them, but look to add something special that makes the bedroom relaxing and enjoyable.

Photo by Monetti Custom Homes

Bathrooms

There are basics that everyone needs in a bathroom – a sink, shower, and toilet. From there the options are up to your needs and wants. Many shared bathrooms or kid's bathrooms have a double sink to make it easier for multiple people to use the bathroom. A vanity with drawers and doors allows for plenty of storage.

Photo by Lombardi Residential   Architecture by PDRdesigns

Upper cabinets can provide additional storage or you can do without them for a less busy, cleaner look. As in the master bath, you can use a half wall to hide the toilet or a separate room. When designing a Jack and Jill bathroom (one that has access from 2 different bedrooms). It is common to have the sinks in the general area and another room for the toilet and shower, allowing maximum usage of the space. For a shared bath, a linen closet is highly recommended as there are many towels and items that need to be accommodated.

Joseph Carranante, CEO of Cara Realtors in Point Pleasant, NJ shared with me his advice of bathrooms and showers versus tubs. "In the majority of homes, the shower gets used far more than the bath tub, as a result there is a trend towards getting rid of tubs completely and going for the spacious shower. While this might suit your personal needs, it's not a great idea when it comes to return on investment (ROI). While modern updated walk in showers are becoming more popular among current buyers, some still want the option to have a bathtub. As a real estate professional, I suggest having at least one bathtub in the house for the most resale value."

Joseph Carranante, CEO, Cara Realtors
606 Arnold Ave. Pt. Pleasant, NJ 08742
732-892-9900
www.cararealtors.com

So what about the finishes in the bathroom? Tile floors are the most popular, but you can also use stone, vinyl, or wood (not recommended due to the moisture in the room, but the tile that looks like wood is very popular). On a low budget there are some vinyl tiles that look great and are easy to install. On a higher end, real stone with an inlay can create an eye catching elegant design.

Moving to the walls, wainscoting is a classic beachy/shore style or a simple tile or painted walls with a wood base is an easy solution.

A note here about base trim in a bathroom; keep in mind that the water supply to the toilet typically comes out about 6" above the floor. This often falls ½ in and ½ out of a base trim whether wood or tile. Consider this early on in the design, so this height can be specified to avoid an ugly cut in the base for the escutcheon plate around the water supply. Speaking of tile details, you may have similar issues at outlets, switches, vanity tops or the backsplash and your mirror heights. Carefully plan out all of these details before finding out at the end that there are conflicts. A little extra design time is well worth the time spent!

Creative Closets

One of the most often heard complaints is a lack of storage space in homes. To make kids closets feel much larger, the first thing to do is remove the sliding or swinging doors and allow it to be open to the room. Paint it the same color as the room or a complimentary color for visual appeal and add double hanging bars. Boys don't need any long hanging items, but girls may need space for longer dresses. Throw in a few cubbies and extra shelves, simple show racks or cubbies at the bottom and you have an efficient, effective layout that adds space to the room and is organized! However, if you can fit in a walk in closet, it allows for much more shelving and closet storage.

Most of the big chain stores have great organizing units, cubbies, and rods that can be mixed and matched for the look you want. For the next level up, contact California Closets or a local cabinetry shop and they can provide all options and accessories to create any look you desire.

With new home building, allow enough space in each bedroom for a walk in closet. This will leave more wall space in the bedroom and

allows the flexibility to create efficient storage in the closet. We have also done center islands in closets or benches for getting dressed. Think of a theme that inspires you, review lots of pictures to get what you like and fits your taste, decide what you want, review lots of pictures to see what you like and what fits your taste, decide what you want and then go for it!

Basement

A basement can be an unfinished space for storage, heating equipment and a water heater or it can be a magnificent addition to the home. When designing new, consider a 9' or 10' height as this will allow for ductwork and pipes to drop below the floor and you will still have plenty of ceiling height. If your property slopes and you can create a walk out basement with glass doors and windows then you can have an awesome space that feels open and airy. Even if your property is not sloped, you can create an open stairway to bring in light and access to the yard.

The basement makes and ideal place for a game room with a pool table, a bar for entertaining and possibly a kitchenette.

Ceiling details will help conceal any ductwork or pipes that drop down and create a unique feeling to your space. If you want to add a bedroom in the basement, keep in mind you will need a window in the bedroom that meets egress codes in case of a fire. For flooring, the most popular choice is carpet, next is hardwood, and last is tile. Carpet is warmer for the northern regions, hardwood is for any region, but make sure you use the type that is pre-engineered and can be glued down over concrete. Tile can be used for any region but works especially well in southern states. A gym is another popular room with an attached full

Photo by PDRdesigns   Theatre by iTEC Consultants

Photo by PDRdesigns

bathroom with a steam shower and possibly a sauna to relax in after a workout.

Looking for a wine tasting room or wine cellar? What better place than this? Add some mahogany display shelving, a table and chairs for friends and you are all set. Some other cool rooms to create in a basement are a gym/workout room which will require higher ceilings for a fan, bikes and treadmills and walls for mirrors. Meditation rooms for peace, tranquility, and time to clear your mind. Sauna rooms for your post workout recovery. A game room with a billiard table and shuffle board table, foosball and a bar is a cool space to hang out.

Keep an open mind as to design options and how to make this level of the house a fun retreat!

Photo by Trademark Design and Build

Photo by Philip Gorrivan, Designer

Lauren Sisler, Sportscaster at Al.com and ESPN, sat down with me to talk about fun rooms. Lauren has interviewed some of the biggest sports stars and shared with me some great ideas she has and has seen regarding game and sports rooms.

A game room starts with comfort, which is subjective to each person's taste. Lauren has been in all kinds of game room suites for athletes and sees the most common component is a place to relax with friends and have fun. This can be accomplished with video gaming systems, foosball table, shuffleboard, tennis and basketball courts. It may not even be "your" sport, just one you love. This is the case with Denny Hamlin, NASCAR driver, who built a 31,000 square foot home on Lake Norman complete with a full basketball court inspired by his good friend and basketball legend, Michael Jordan.

Lauren has her ideal room all planned out already and here are some of her "must have" items. Lauren wants it to be comfortable and relaxed where friends can sit back on couches, watch movies, or play video games on the big theater screen. What games? Her favorites are the old school Nintendo, Sega Genesis, and N64 for Mario Kart of course. A bar would be nearby with all kinds of sports drinks and a Slurpee machine! Being a former Captain of the Rutgers University gymnastics team, a trampoline room complete with basketball nets and foam pits would be her main attraction. Some of her highlight career moments would be displayed on the walls with pictures of her interviewing athletes and coaches.

One of her favorite interviews was the one she set up with Charles Barkley and Nick Saban to talk basketball. She was amused when she presented Charles with a framed picture of the event and he asked her if she could have Nick Saban sign it. So yes, even sports stars like autographs! Having the ability to capture and present moments like this would complete her game room. Lauren's advice – Think big, make it fun, and most importantly make it you!

Specialty Rooms

I've discussed a few specialty rooms previously, but here I wanted to list rooms that are not typical in every house but may be a great addition to your new home.

- Pool room for an indoor lap pool or elaborate larger pool
- Theater Room for that movie night experience anytime you want. These can be as decorative as your budget allows with multitier seating, custom trim, fabric covered walls and in wall speakers. Consider a good soundproofing system to isolate this room from overpowering the rest of the house.
- A bowling alley for family fun nights.
- A golf simulator room equipped with a full screen and ample space for a full swing is great for the avid golfer!
- An indoor basketball court will require much higher ceilings.

Photo by iTec Consultants

- An ice rink requires specialized construction and an HVAC system and condenser for the ice.

- A gun room/trophy room can be super creative and have themes for all of the different environments where you have hunted and want to display your animal mounts.

- Sports Memorabilia room for the sports lover to display trophies or jerseys, helmets, or any other items you like to display.

Laundry Room

When my children were 10, 13, 16, and 23, I was continually overloaded with laundry and decided that a new rule was needed in the house. Everyone does their own laundry! Being recently divorced, there was only so much I could do in a day. I showed them how to do it and from then on they were each responsible for their own clothes.

Luckily, my laundry room has enough room for the washer, dryer, cabinets, and ample floor space. This helps with the multiple piles of clothes that tend to accumulate. Located off of the mud room, which is adjacent to the kitchen, it allows for a quick, easy "pop-in" to switch loads as needed. To me, this is an ideal setup – not only are my children doing their own laundry, but the location and size of the room work perfectly.

Other items to consider for a laundry room, that I have seen on clients' wish lists, are an oversized low sink/tub for washing the dog, a large sink, and window ledge or cabinets for planting activities. The flooring should be a stone, tile, or similar surface, and if located above a finished basement or on the second floor I recommend a floor drain under the washer/dryer in case of leaks or overflows.

The laundry room is morphing into a multifunction laundry, mud room, craft room, locker room, or gardening room space all in one.

Craft rooms alone are becoming more popular with cabinetry to store everything, a counter to work on and a table to create crafts, sewing or scrapbooking.

Photo by PDRdesigns

Mud Room

Similar to the laundry room, the Mud Room is generally near the kitchen and a side door or entrance from the garage. The size of this room depends upon what amenities you would like. Some owners will combine the laundry and mud room to save space. As washers and dryers have become better-looking, this option has become more popular.

At a minimum, you will need wall space for a few hooks for jackets.

If space permits, a coat closet and a bench with storage below for boots and shoes, with hooks above for hats and scarves, will serve you well. Some people want lockers for kids to be able to keep their gear off the floor.

A cubby above the bench allows for baskets with extra hats and gloves. I like this wall treatment and renovated my own mud room in a similar fashion after sports bags, hockey sticks, soccer cleats, and backpacks ruined the sheetrock corners one too many times!

The flooring should be durable and able to handle wet items from rain or snow. I recommend a tile or stone floor. In my house I built a pocket door to separate the mud room from the kitchen for when I need to close the room off due to excessive child-related mess! If you have an attached

garage, some of those bench, cubby, or hanging spaces may be incorporated there as well, to ease the burden of "stuff" that can easily clutter up a typical mudroom.

Garage

I designed and built my house sixteen years ago with the intention of adding a detached garage the following year. I still don't have a garage, but I get along just fine without it! I have a large basement, and a shed for outdoor storage, and these suit my needs just fine. **Although on those snowy, icy, below-zero mornings… that's when I truly wish I had a garage!**

My grandfather had a small detached garage that never had a car in it, but housed meticulously kept tools and a workbench. It was a treat to be allowed in, to see the organization and the beautiful tools, to smell the earthy, woodsy air. That smell still brings me back to those summer days with my grandfather. His tools now line the shelves in my office as a

daily reminder of where I came from. Whatever your purpose is for the garage – attached or detached, for cars or for tools – here are design factors to consider. Where do you want it located? Generally you want to place it on the same side of the

> **TIP:** Some towns or Homeowners Associations have rules regarding the garage doors facing the street, so make sure to check that during the planning phase.

house as the mud room and kitchen. How many cars do you want it to hold, and will you need extra space for other vehicles such as jet skis, tractors, or ATVs? Do you need room and the proper electrical setup for a work area or even an extra refrigerator? Is there enough space for large garbage and recycling cans? All these items will help you to determine the size needed. Will this be detached or attached from the house, set back or pulled forward? Do you want to see the garage doors when you pull in or should they be facing the side yard?

Photo and Architecture by PDRdesigns

Will you be installing a lift for storing additional cars up high? Do you want a concrete floor as the finish, or will you install an epoxy coating over it or carpeting? (Yes, I have had clients who want their garages to feel like finished rooms!) If you live in a colder climate, do you want a gas heater or in-floor heat with insulation in the walls and sheetrock on the walls.

Knowing your use of the space simplifies the design process and gives you confidence that you have considered all of the options and made the correct choices.

8 DESIGN OPTIONS

Lighting Design

The lighting of a space makes a huge impact on how it feels and your experience. One of first rules to follow is to have ample lighting in the room. The second rule is to light up the correct surfaces.

Ceiling mounted fixtures will spread light over a larger area. Recessed lights come in various sizes and shine light onto walls or downward to the floor. Wall sconces spread light up, down, or out. Track lights can be decorative and enable light to be directed to where it is needed. Rope lights enable light to be flexible and decorative, and provide a soothing accent.

> *The Details are not the details, they make the design.*
>
> — *Charles Eames*

Think about how you want a space to feel and what type of fixture will help you create that feel. Utilizing a lighting designer will allow you to get exactly what you want in a space as they understand all of the different light fixtures, styles, light output of each, and how to provide lighting that is specific to the tasks needed in each room and the mood you want to feel.

Robert Newell, lighting designer, and I caught up to share thoughts on what makes up a quality lighting plan.

"The best time to bring a lighting designer onto your design team is at the end of the schematic design phase. This allows them to help you in the creation of details that will get the most out of your light locations. Typically your architect will recommend a lighting designer as they will introduce you to option that you may not know existed. I stress the quality of illumination with my clients, not the quantity. All rooms have different tasks performed in them and therefore need to be it differently. I strive to capture the feel of the space by creatively utilizing the walls, ceilings and floors to capture the light. Indirect lighting provides an ambient glow, which adds immensely to the visual interest in a room. This is what creates the atmosphere that the client desires. After understanding how my client will use each space and what the family routine is, I provide lighting plans, details and full specifications as to what light fixtures to use. Hanging fixtures are noted, but typically your interior designer will select those items.

The interior and exterior are designed around what each unique client and site condition warrants. Some clients call me in for a room addition or remodel and some utilize me for a complete house and landscape lighting plan."

Robert Newell Lighting Design
654 North Ave. W
Westfield, NJ 07090
908-654-9304
Robertnewelllightingdesign.com

Landscape Design

Landscape design takes into its scope much more than just plants and trees. It also covers the driveway, gates, decorative walls, pathways, trellis, pools, decks and outdoor entertaining areas. Typical projects begin with design and material selection and finish with the correct installation of these materials.

To begin this process, write out your dream ideas and then prioritize those items. Budget is a key component here so having a priority list of the most important items is a great help in determining the scope of the project.

Putting together a team of designers early on in your project will enable you to gain from everyone's input and creating your dream home.

Howard Roberts, owner of Liquidscapes, a Landscape Design and Build Company, talks about the 3 principles he bases his company on and how to get started with your project.

"I formulate my company based on 3 principles; Creating great design, using appropriate materials, and executing with precision, all done consistently. Applying this methodology has given us continued success, demonstrated by time and happy clients, which are our ultimate measures of success or failure in business.

The design process is all about embracing the journey and exploring your options. Our goal is to inform and educate our clients, so that they are in a position of strength to make sound decisions for this investment of time and money.

We never compromise our process, methods or standards. Having been in the business 40 years, we know what brings the results our clients expect and you can look back at all of our projects to see that they have stood the test of time.

Similar to a Board of Directors, we suggest assembling a team of designers around a project so that all disciplines are integrated into the overall vision. This includes the architect, builder, landscape architect, pool builder and landscape contractors. At Liquidscapes, we use a comprehensive approach as we are landscape architects, pool builders, and landscape contractors all assembled into one company to provide everything from the "Big Picture" view to the final installation. Prior to meeting our clients, we ask them to assemble a wish list, in order of priority and to provide images to help communicate their thoughts. The other 2 required items are a site survey, showing the existing site conditions and a budget set for what you are planning to do. The goal is to have an efficient 1st meeting and to be able to balance your wants and expectations with your budget.

This is how we think of our design process. We think of design as a funnel. Start with the wide rim, the Big Picture, and get specific as the design progresses. The program is first laying out all the items you want incorporated and how they best work on the site, taking into account property setbacks, drainage restrictions, sun location and circulation or flow of people.

Next, consider materials to use that will tie new and existing pieces together and then scale of elements to make sure everything is

Photo and Design Construction by Liquidscapes

proportional. The plants are like the furniture in a room and will be the last piece of the design scheme.

Liquidscapes
313 Pittstown Rd. #665
Pittstown, NJ 08867
Phone: 908-752-9650
Email: ***howard@liquidscapes.net***
Website: ***www.liquidscapes.net***

Photo and Design Construction by Liquidscapes

Integrated Technology

Families today are reliant on technology. Incorporating technology into a project is no longer an option, it is considered a necessity. A great way to test this theory is to unplug your router one day thus shutting down wifi / internet to the house. You will hear immediately from all family members "Internet is down!" That is just one example of how critical technology is to everyone today for both staying productive and relaxing. With the most recent advent of smart phones, tablets and wireless devices, everyone wants to have a robust internet signal throughout the house as they do not want to be eating into their cellular data surfing the web at home when they could do so from a properly designed Wifi network.

Being educated during the design phase as to what technology options are available today is very important. Systems such as Distributed Music, Lighting and Shade Control, Surveillance and Security as well as Sub Systems integration to HVAC, Garage and Entry Doors and Pool and Spa Control are just some of the many technology offerings which should be discussed before starting construction. Incorporating these systems will impact other trades work (electrician, cabinet maker, HVAC contractor, etc), having everything planned out in advance allows the homeowner to understand how these options will tie-in other trades and ultimately enhance the enjoyment of their new home.

Joe McNeill, from iTEC Consultants discusses how important client education is in an excerpt below.

"We start by educating our client's as to what technologies are available today and then see what resonates with them. The time invested before a project begins is integral to the satisfaction of our clients and trade partners, we want everyone to "be on the same page". iTEC Consultants engineers, installs and services systems such as Wireless Networks, Distributed Music and Video, Multipurpose Media Rooms and Theaters, Telephone / Intercom Systems, Surveillance and Security and Subsystem Integrations such as Gates, Driveway sensors, Heating and Cooling sensors, etc."

Joe shares how important it is for each client to have the opportunity to understand the value of prewiring their homes to support the systems they may get upon moving in or would want to add down the road. Proactive communication throughout the design, construction and aftercare process is of the utmost importance to each member of the iTEC team.

iTEC Consultants
101 Park Avenue, Union Beach, NJ 07735
Joe McNeill
Phone: 732-710 9086
Email: *jmcneill@iTECconsultants.com*
Website: *www.iTECconsultants.com*

Photo and Design by iTec Consultants

9 HIRING A CONTRACTOR

A good countenance is a letter of recommendation.

— Henry Ford

Finding a good general contractor that will be able to build your project in the timeframe and budget that you would like is important. In order to find a good general contractor, there are many sources for information. Your architect is the best person to consult for a recommendation, then ask friends and family to see who has built a similar project and who they used. I will stress similar project as you do not want the guy that does tile work to be the general contractor for a new house. Find someone that is a general contractor to fill that role. Look online for contractors in your area or ask at the local lumberyard for names of people that they deal with on a regular basis. You can also check out websites such as NARI – National Association of the Remodeling Industry or the NAHB – The National Association of Home Builders. Drive around town and see what companies have signs out at houses similar to yours.

Questions to ask your potential contractor on the phone or in person:

- Have you built a project similar to this before and can I see pictures of those projects?
- Who will be running my job on a day to day basis?
- How do you bill for your services?
- Can I speak to references from current and past jobs? (At least 3 recent projects)
  - When you talk to references, ask them how responsive the contractor was, if there were any time, quality or cost concerns, would they use them again, if there were any warranty issues getting the contractor back from repairs?
- How long have you been running this company or how long has this company been around?
- Have you owned any other construction companies?
- How many projects do you have going on at one time?
- How long do you expect this project to take?

Make sure the contractor you are interviewing is licensed and insured. Contact your state Department of Consumer Affairs to see what licenses are required and then verify that the contractor has those licenses in current standing. Obtain a copy of their insurance coverage to be sure you will be covered if there is a problem once construction begins.

This first group of questions can be an over the phone interview designed to see how you feel about the company initially. Pay close attention to how responsive they are in this phase. How quickly do they respond to emails or phone calls, are they on time when you schedule meetings? Are they friendly and courteous? If you don't have a good feeling at this point in the relationship, I suggest you find someone else to interview.

Your next step is the face to face interview. Depending upon your project, you may want to meet at your house, for a remodel, or their office, for a new home. Wherever you are more comfortable is fine. The purpose of this meeting is to see how you connect, look at work they have done and talk about your project.

If you already have your architectural plans at this point, then you can review those and discuss rough pricing to get some guidelines and make sure your project is reasonable. Meet with 3 or 4 contractors at this point to get a feel for how well they communicate with you. Clear communication and trust are essential as you will be investing a lot of time and money with this person. Ask them about your project and have them walk you through how the process will unfold, what they will do, what you will have to do, how long it will take when you will be informed of items that you need to select and who will keep track of all of the selections that are made throughout the process. A hint here- Typically, the better contractors are much more organized than others. Have a notepad with you at all times and write things down as you make decisions. Follow up with an email clarifying what was decided to avoid any possible confusion. I have seen many times a wrong door is ordered or a wrong color of an item arrives on site due to a simple miscommunication. Even if it is a simple issue to fix, it will cost you lost time and depending on the item, it may cost a lot of money to change.

Ask them to walk thru an existing project. Look to see if the site is clean, are the workers courteous? Are materials protected properly from damage?

By now you should know if this is a person and a company that you would like to work with. If they are, then ask them to provide a price for your project. Ask them to break it out in a line item format, so that you can compare pricing with other proposals.

Make sure that a financial schedule is discussed and you understand exactly when payments will be required and how much they will be. Payments are generally progress driven and will occur after stages are complete, such as footing and foundation, framing, setting window and exterior doors, roofing, siding, mechanical electrical and plumbing installations, insulating and sheetrock, flooring, interior doors and trim, and painting. Depending on the scope of your project there may be more or less milestones for payment. If there are a set # of payments then it may be broken into 10% to start, 3 payments of 25% each and then 15% at the end and when all punch list items are completed. Every aspect of this is negotiable so feel free to adjust this so that you are comfortable with the agreements.

> **TIP:** See the appendix or go to www.pdrdesigns.com to request an excel file that you can use for an example of a break down I use when putting construction costs together.

When you receive pricing from your contractors, sit with them again to be sure you understand what is included in the price and what is excluded. Once you have done that, you can then fairly evaluate the different prices you have. If you received a price that is way different than the others, be wary. Most likely they have not included some items or used different materials or less skilled labor than the others.

Find out what types of warranties are offered on labor and materials and make sure you have all of this spelled out in writing.

Don't make your decision based solely on price. You typically get what you pay for, so be sure you are comfortable with the person and company that you are selecting. It is worth paying more to get the company that you believe will do the best job.

Understand the contract fully before signing anything. The next chapter explains the contract in depth, so let's read on!

Before

A full scale addition and alteration by PDRdesigns turned this small cape style home into the client's dream home!

After

10 THE CONSTRUCTION CONTRACT

Let's start with the 2 basic types of Construction Contracts and the difference in each. A fixed fee or lump sum contract is a set amount of money for a specific job scope. A cost plus time and material contract can be set up as an hourly fee plus materials and an overhead and profit percentage added in or it can have fixed subcontractor costs plus an overhead and profit percentage. Whichever form of contract you choose, make sure these items are included. (Many states have laws regarding what information must be included in the contract so look into it to make sure what you are signing has the correct information that your state requires).

In general, these are the items to be included in your contract.

- Your name and address, the project location and your contractors name, address and phone number.
- A specific scope of work explaining what work is to be performed, what materials are to be used and any allowances that are included.

A common area that causes confusion for owners and frustration for contractors is the Allowance items in a contract. Simply put, an Allowance is a set price that has been "Allowed" for an item when the exact item selections and

options have not been made. An allowance is common for items such as cabinetry, countertops, flooring, tile, plumbing fixtures, door hardware, and front
and side entry doors if they have not been selected prior to getting prices.
Allowances work like this: tile is shown on the plans, but the exact size, color,
style and layout may not have been determined yet, so the contractor allows
a price in the bid of $6 per square foot for material and $6 per square foot for
installation. When you go tile shopping, if you choose a tile that will cost less
than the $6 per square foot, you will get a credit back. If you choose a material
that costs more than the $6 per square foot, then you have to pay the differ-
ence above the allowed price in the quote.

Make sure when reviewing the bids and speaking to the contractors
that the allowances are enough to cover the basics of what you want. There
should not be an allowance of $300 for a door that will cost a minimum of
$2,000. Make sure you ask that the allowances given in dollars allow for a
comparable product to what is shown.

Tim Cross of Merrick Construction told me recently of a story
about an owner that told him his price was much higher than another
contractor. When Tim sat down with the owner to compare estimates,
they discovered that the other contractor did not include the correct
amount for allowances. Clear communication and trustworthiness made
the owner realize that Tim and Merrick Construction was the right
builder for them and loved the job when it was complete!

Merrick Construction
524 Prospect Ave B, Little Silver, NJ 07739
732-758-0404
www.merrickbuilders.com

These allowances can vary greatly from one contractor to another, so be
sure to look at these items to see what each person is providing.

- A total cost or what the hourly rates are and what the percent
  markup will be on the overall bill for Overhead and Profit.

- How and when payments will be made. At the completion of certain stages? At the beginning of certain stages? Percent of progress

completed? Which items are included as billable items- nails, saw blades, tool or scaffold rentals, glue, etc.

- What is the construction schedule and how long is the project anticipated to take from beginning to end? When will it begin?
- A contract document list, showing all Architectural, site, and designer plans that were used to bid on the project. These should have dates on the documents as well in case changes are made after the bid is completed.
- Construction responsibilities- who obtains permits from the town, who is responsible for inspections when will decisions be requested of the owner and what time frame are they expected to reply.
- If there is a disagreement between parties will the case go to arbitration or a trial court (always request an Arbitration clause if one is not in there)
- What insurance is the contractor going to provide and is the owner required to provide any additional insurance? (Note: Check with your homeowners policy on this item) (Extra Note: Insurance companies DO NOT cover faulty workmanship so choose your contractor carefully!)
- How can work be stopped or terminated if the parties are unhappy?
- What is substantial completion and what is expected at final completion?

Some clients will request a time frame with liquidated damages if the contract is not completed on time, however a Liquidated Damages clause is almost impossible to enforce, so leave it out, it won't help you.

- How will change orders be billed and what is the procedure for approving additional costs? (You don't want to be stuck at the end with a long list of change orders that you did not previously have pricing for.)
- Will release of liens be signed as the job progresses?
- What is the process for generating a punch list (a list of items that still need to be corrected or finished) at the end of the project and in what time frame will they be completed?

When reviewing the contract, you can always ask for a clarification of an item or revision to it. Some of these items may not apply to you and your project. There may be additional items that should be in there based on your locality.

In order to accurately review costs, be sure to understand each item and look line by line to see that the contract you are comparing it to is the same. If numbers are different find out what the difference is.

This is your house, your project and you need to understand exactly what you are getting before signing anything.

A contractor telling you something is included is good, but having it clearly in writing will avoid any miscommunications later and therefore allow for less problems and a smoother construction process.

Joe Lepore, Esq. of Lepore and Luizzi, Attorneys at Law, stresses the importance of understanding the construction contract.

"Understand the terms of the contract and even have a lawyer review for you. Make sure you know what happens in the event of a dispute as most contracts now have arbitration clauses in them. Make sure there are end dates and beginning dates and verify what type of contract it is, cost plus or fixed price. Make sure the contractor identifies the product used so you can verify when it's delivered or installed. Take photos through-out the project. Make sure every change order is in writing and that you sign each one. Just become as knowledgeable as you can, get to know the project manager so that he can answer any questions you have along the way. The house you're building is probably your biggest investment so being informed and knowledgeable is your duty."

Joe Lepore, Esq.
Lepore and Luizzi Attorneys at Law
Brick, New Jersey, NJ 08723
Phone: 732-920-5500
www.leporeluizzi.com

11 THE PROS AND CONS OF BECOMING YOUR OWN GENERAL CONTRACTOR

"Living a life is like constructing a building: If you start wrong, you'll end wrong"

— Maya Angelou

For those adventurous owners that would like to be their own general contractor I will devote this chapter to educating and cautioning you about this process. If you have the time and knowledge to perform this aspect of the job, it is a fantastic opportunity, however it is also a very daunting task should not be undertaken by those unfamiliar with the construction process.

There are advantages (Pros) and disadvantages (Cons) to becoming your own General Contractor and I would like you to fully understand them prior to making this decision. For most people, the #1 reason they would like to be their own General Contractor is to save money. They figure they can save 10-30% and therefore stretch their budget further. In theory, this sounds like a fantastic idea, but in reality this does not always happen. It can happen and work out very well and you're so glad you did it when it's over, but in general, the comment I hear is "I would never do that again".

Let's start with what you will have to do as a General Contractor you will be responsible for overall job cleanliness (yes, each subcontractor should clean up after themselves, but this doesn't always happen). Jobsite Safety – did someone dig a hole that needs to be protected, are the doors locked each night, is material stacked where it can fall or break or hurt someone? Scheduling – is all material ordered on time, are subcontractors available and scheduled to keep the job flowing. Inspections – are you onsite to meet inspectors or are your subcontractors handling all inspections? Deliveries – will you unload the delivery truck when it arrives and be there to sign or pay the invoices and check all material to make sure it is correct and not damaged? When material arrives early who protects it on the job and moves it on jobsite or moves it when it is in the way?

Soooo... Here are the basics.

Advantages:

- Save money when well executed.
- Save time when you are on top of it.
- Get exactly what you want since you pick all the materials used.
- Learn the process better for your next project.
- Bragging rights with friends! ☺

Disadvantages:

- Potential to lose money if not well executed.
- Requires an enormous amount of time and flexibility.
- You are responsible if anything goes wrong.
- Potential to be dragged out over the allotted time frame.

Now you have to decide. Going back to the beginning of this chapter, I said if you have time and knowledge, those are the key ingredients. Having family or friends that are in construction doesn't count. You have to have the knowledge and time available to commit to your project. Many people will tell me, well, I can do tile and trim and hang sheetrock and that sounds awesome BUT do you have time to do all that for this scale of a project schedule? This is where many people fall behind and then way too late, decide to call in help when they are already way behind schedule and over costs.

Here are some other items you need to know if you choose to proceed.

The key to running a job is communication.

Learning how to effectively communicate with building inspectors, subcontractors and suppliers will ease your frustrations. Listening to others is of utmost importance throughout the process. This does not mean you need to act on everything you are told, but listening to different thoughts or ways to accomplish a task will help you to weed out good information from bad information. Sometimes it is good to tell others that you do not know about a particular product or process in order have it fully explained to you.

This book provides a summary of the tasks that need to take place in order to successfully complete your project. As your own general contractor you will be the one performing these tasks. You may or may not want to do your own design work and depending upon the scope of work to be done and the state your project is located in, the local building department may allow you to submit your own construction drawings. The International Residential Building Code allows homeowners to submit their own plans for construction, but many times the Building Department will require a licensed architect to sign and seal the structural portions of the plans to ensure the building will stand up.

They tend to frown upon houses collapsing, sagging, catching fire or any other health and safety issues!

The best way to ascertain if you are allowed to submit your own drawings is to visit the local building department and tell them what you are planning to do and ask them what you are allowed to submit and what the various requirements are. Very often I find that it depends how a question is asked as to what answer is received. Example:

Joey, a local homeowner, calls his local building department and asks Julia, the young lady with the sweet voice that has answered the phone, if he is allowed to build an addition. She states that yes, additions are allowed in town and they must comply with the zoning laws.. He tells her thank you, hangs up and proceeds to begin construction because he has checked the zoning and he is within the building setback requirements. A few days later Brad, the large surly inspector comes by and says "STOP!", and issues Joey a fine and summons for building without a permit. Joey is taken aback and explains that he spoke to the building department and they told him that he could add on to his house.

This is an extreme example, but serves the purpose of describing how a miscommunication takes place. Asking the correct questions would have clarified the answers. Many times people will not volunteer information and it is up to you to ask the correct questions to get the information that is desired. If Joey had asked instead if there were any rules about adding on to a house he would have learned there were. Don't be afraid to ask questions and keep asking until you understand the answers.

So now that we understand the importance of communication, what else is needed? I will outline the basic steps and give a brief summary of how each item will affect you, the General Contractor.

Scheduling

This is the most time consuming and important item of the job!
If you are acting as your own general contractor, you are responsible for when materials and subcontractors show up on the job. With all of the various activities, staying on top of this item and communicating with the material suppliers and subcontractors is essential. If your wonderful trim contractor shows up to install the trim and it has not arrived yet he may charge you for wasted time or leave your job to go to another job and not be back for a week. Either scenario is not good; but what is worse is when the wrong material is delivered, you didn't check it, he installs it and you have to pay to rip it out, pay for more correct material and pay to have it installed again. (and yes, this has happened).

When you hire contractors and subcontractors make sure you understand when their phase of the work begins and what needs to be completed for them to come in to perform their task. Also find out how much notice they need to schedule your job. Try to keep the contractors informed as to how your project is progressing so they can plan accordingly. If when you hired them, you had anticipated electrical wiring to start installation on June 10th, but due to delays, it seems more like June 24th, then call or email to let them know. This allows them to schedule other work and still keep you on the schedule.

A note of caution about scheduling: If you do not push the contractors to start when you would like them to, then the job will be hopelessly behind schedule. It starts simple with a contractor's request such as, "can we get there Thursday instead of Monday?", but Thursday becomes Saturday and then a week is lost and that throws off the next trade. This can also affect material deliveries and now materials are in the way and need to be moved.

Scheduling is the most difficult task you will need to accomplish and it is essential to keep a written timeline showing each phase of the project and when it will occur. This allows you to have a beginning date, a finish date and know when all the other tasks need to be performed to stay within that schedule. Time is money and the sooner you can get completed, the sooner you can relax and enjoy the fruit of your labor. I see many jobs that people undertake themselves stretch on weeks and months behind schedule due either to a lack of understanding as to what needs to take place when or not having materials and contractors lined up at the appropriate times. If you are ordering materials, find out how far in advance you need to order to give the product time to be shipped and arrive on site.

The number one reason people fall behind schedule that I see is lack of knowledge of when things should happen and what needs to be done to get to the next step. This is why asking a question is so important. It is ok to tell people that you do not know something. I have always believed that you will appear much more intelligent seeking knowledge than you will pretending that you know it all already.

Don't be afraid to ask!

Even if you think you know about timeframes and scheduling, confirm this with the contractors you speak to, in case they do something differently or there is some bit of information you did not know about.

Here is an example of what not to do with scheduling:

After speaking to Fred, from Fred's Custom Framing, you decide that you would like to use his company and his proposal is within your budget. You tell Fred, that you would like to work with him and will call him when you are ready. You did not sign the contract yet as you wanted to wait until it was time to start. When you complete the masonry portion and are ready to start framing the next day, you call Fred to see what time he can be on site tomorrow morning. He says that he has not heard from you in a month and that he is tied up on another job for another three weeks. Can you spell D E L A Y ??

Here is an example of how this should have been handled:

Upon deciding that you would like to use Fred's Custom Framing, you sign his contract and write in that a deposit (if one is required) will be paid about a week before the job begins and that the anticipated start date is July 16th. Now you ask Fred how much notice he needs to order material and be on site to start. He says to call two weeks before you are ready for him, to make sure you are still on schedule. To follow up, you call Fred when the mason begins to let him know that the job has started and you anticipate the mason will be done by July 16th, which is 4 weeks from now and to confirm that he is still available to start on that date. Following up again in two weeks you confirm that all is on schedule and you anticipate seeing him on July 16th. I would take this a step further and call again in 1 week to confirm all is ready in one week to start and if a check is due that he can stop by to get it or you can mail it.

In the above examples, you can see that a few minutes of phone calls may save you weeks of delay. Now imagine if all of the contractors had the same communication and scheduling problems! Do you think the project will stay on target?

Communication and scheduling are key aspects of running a smooth job!

Ordering Materials

Most likely there will be materials that you are ordering directly for the contractors to install. These may include tile, plumbing fixtures, door hardware, windows or a whole variety of other products, depending upon how much you want to get involved in the process. It is easier to have the contractor order materials, but then you will be paying a markup on those materials. On the other hand if you order material and it is damaged or you ordered the wrong items, you may be charged extra for time wasted due to material issues.

Here is a list of typical materials used on a job and who generally orders what:

Masonry / Concrete:

Mason contractor will order all materials needed.

Framing:

General Contractor, which is you, orders material based upon a lumber list provided by the Framing Contractor. Windows and doors that are to be installed are also ordered by you. Confirm who orders nails, screws, window wrap for preparing the window openings, etc.

Roofing:

Roofing contractor supplies and installs underlayment, flashing and shingles for a complete job.

Siding:

Siding contractor supplies and installs all building paper, flashing, vents, siding and fascia boards as needed.

Heating / Air Conditioning:

All units and ductwork supplied by contractor for a complete job. If custom vent covers are wanted, these may be ordered by you, but clarify this with the contractor.

Plumbing:

All pipes, fittings, vents supplied by the contractor. You can order toilets, sinks, shower valves and faucets, but your contractor may receive better pricing on these items and it may be easier for him to order so that no parts are forgotten about. Discuss this item with your plumber.

Electrical:

All wiring, panels and recessed lights are supplied by the contractor. You will be responsible for ordering ceiling fans, wall sconces, ceiling mounted and pendant lights which the electrician will install.

Insulation:

Insulation contractor supplies all material.

Gypsum Board (Sheetrock as some call it, although this is actually a brand name):

Gypsum Board contractor supplies all material.

Interior Doors and Trim:

This can be either one. Contractor may get better pricing and know better supply yards, but clarify who is responsible for material. Nails and glue supplied by installer. Make sure you know what you are getting- solid or hollow Manufacturer, style, hinge style and color.

Carpet:

Installer supplies all material.

Hardwood Flooring:

Installer generally supplies material, glue, nails, but flooring can be supplied by you if you want to shop around for better pricing or exotic woods. Clarify with contractor.

Kitchen & Bath Cabinets and Countertops:

If you are using a cabinet showroom, they will supply and install all cabinets and tops. If you would like to design the layout, shop cabinets and countertop pricing, then you can supply these items and find a contractor to install your material. I recommend using a shop that will supply and install as there are so many variables with cabinets and tops. Even on good jobs there are a few glitches, so think about this item carefully.

Door Hardware and Bathroom Accessories:

If you purchase from a specialty shop, they may offer installation, otherwise you can purchase the items you want and the trim contractor or cabinet installer (sometimes this is the same person) can install them.

Paint:

Painting contractor supplies all material.

Those are the basics to give you a quick understanding. Now choose carefully and think twice about acting as your own General Contractor. As a rule of thumb, I don't recommend it! But then again, this is your project, your time, your money and your decisions.

12 PERMITS

Start where you are, use what you have, do what you can.

— Arthur Ashe

Now that the Architectural Plans are completed, signed, and sealed and you've selected your General Contractor, it's time to file for your building permit. This can be done by you, the homeowner, but is typically performed by your General Contractor or by an expeditor or your Architect depending on the region. I strongly recommend not filing for this yourself. It can be a long frustrating experience with many trips back and forth.

Permitting starts in the Town Zoning Department where the proper paperwork will be filled out and submitted. If your project meets all of the towns zoning requirements for property line setbacks. Height, use, etc. then the zoning department reviews it and approves it. If you do not meet all of the zoning requirements you will have to make and application to the zoning

NOTE: Some smaller towns may have a joint Planning Board and Zoning Board. As part of the site investigation by your site engineer and Architect, you will already know whether you need a Zoning Variance or not, so there is no guessing or hoping at this point in the process.

board of adjustment to as for approval to so something that is not in line with the towns rules.

As part of the zoning permit, the site plan will also be reviewed by the Engineering Department (again this may be a joint department in some towns) to make sure you comply with Lot coverage, drainage, curb cuts and any other requirements the local department has. All of these items are addressed on your Plot Plan or Survey.

Depending where you are located, other agencies may need to be contacted as well. Other permits that may be required: If you do not have a city water and sewer and you need a well and septic system, then the local Health Department will need to review the Septic Design done by your Engineer and approve this prior to submitting to the town Zoning Department.

If you live on the water or near a stream, pond, marsh, ocean, lagoon, or bay you will be restricted by the Department of Environmental Protection (DEP). This is a well intentioned Government Organization that has gotten totally out of control and spends more time creating regulations than they do actually helping the environment. As with the Health Department, this Permit will need to be approved prior to submitting for a Zoning Permit.

Designing projects in other states and speaking to other Architects around the country, I recommend you ask your Architect, Engineer, and

Town Zoning Department what other Agencies Approvals may be required for your specific location. These listed are the most common that people experience.

Back to the Permit Process … Once Zoning has been approved, we are on to the Building Departments. Some towns require the submittal package be picked up from Zoning and brought to the Building Department. Other towns will transfer the file inter office from Zoning to Building. Either way, after your package is in the Building Department, each separate department or subcode official will have to review it. It typically goes something like this: The plans are placed on the Building Department Official's desk, where he will review it in the order in which it was received. When he reviews it, he will either write up a list of items that are unclear, incorrect, or missing or he will approve it and pass it on to the next official. Let's say it goes to the Fire subcode Official's desk next where it waits for him to complete the files he received before yours and then he moves on to yours. Likewise, he either makes comments or approves it and it moves to Plumbing, repeat process, then Electrical, repeat process, and then back to the front desk where they either write up the approvals and contact you or they write up the rejection list from all of the subcode officials notes, and issue that list to you. At this point if it is approved, your General Contractor will get a check from you for the amount due and pick up the permit and begin construction or you will give the rejection list to your Architect and General Contractor and they correct or adjust information as needed and they resubmit to the Building Department where it will go back to each of the desks as needed to get more comments or an approval.

Once you have all Subcode Officials comments satisfied and you have paid the required Permit fees, it's time to start Building!!

Depending on the scope of the project and how busy the local Building Department is, permits may take a couple of weeks or even a couple of months to obtain. If you are dealing with Federal or State Agencies prior to submitting to the local building department, these agencies may take many months to approve. Be sure to understand what permits will be required so that you understand the fees you are dealing with as well as the estimated time frames.

Having this knowledge will help you to set realistic expectations and not be frustrated by the process as it unfolds.

13 CONSTRUCTION – THE PROCESS OF BUILDING

It's a blessing for something to finally start happening for us. The process was pretty smooth.

— Paul Taylor

Now that all of the design is complete and you have your permits, the actual construction can begin! This is a monumental task that will be made easier by knowing what should happen and when.

After all of the planning, now you get to the fun part, the part where you begin to SEE your dreams come to life!

The first order of business will be to clear the land. This can be through demolishing an existing building or clearing trees or grading the terrain. If there is nothing to clear or demolish then hop right into the next step.

Laying out the new addition or house on the land is done by the contractor for simple additions or a land surveyor for a large addition or new home. They put wood stakes in the ground to show where the corners are for the new structure so it gets built in the correct location.

Digging for footings is next and this can be digging a basement or a crawl space or simply footings for a concrete slab on grade construction. (Note: If you are building up in the air on wood pilings, then they would be driven now.

Wood Pilings driven and cut off at grade

Concrete grade beam formed over helical piling caps

Concrete grade beam after pouring

If you are building on wood pilings with a concrete grade beam then the pilings will be driven 1st and then the footings dug.

I love the next step which is forming the footings and installing the steel reinforcing. This is the base, the foundations, and what supports everything and the steel looks really cool when it's done right. After a footing inspection from the town, you are ready to pour concrete!

After the footings are in place its time for the foundation walls. The most common foundation wall construction types are:

1. Concrete masonry units (CMU) also referred to as Block or Cinder block (although they don't use cinder to make the blocks anymore).

2. a poured concrete wall where they set reinforcing steel and forms and then fill it with concrete to form the wall.

3. a Superior Wall System, which is concrete walls built offsite and then brought in and assembled onsite in 1 day (talk about a quick system!)

Depending what system you are using, blocks will be laid or walls will be formed or just set in place with the superior wall systems but either way, your foundation is beginning! When the foundation is complete, the surveyor will come out to survey and make sure it is in the correct spot and at the right height. This information goes to the town, they inspect again and we are on to framing.

Superior Wall Foundation system in place

Piles and piles of wood are delivered, the framing crew grabs some boards, lays out the sill plate on the foundation and starts framing the first floor. Joists are laid, your plywood subfloor is glued down and walls are assembled. These get stood up, the second floor is framed and sheathed and again walls are built and stood up. Now the ceiling is set, rafters set in place and the whole house or addition can be sheathed (this means the plywood is installed on the roof and walls).

OMG it looks like a house now!

Moving right along to a sheathing inspection from the town and then the roofing is installed, windows and doors get set in the openings and siding can begin! **Now it is taking shape!**

It's at this point that the project feels like it slows down as the mechanical ductwork, the plumbing pipes, and the electrical wiring are all installed. These take time and you won't see as much daily progress apparent at this time. Also, at this stage would be the installation of various subsystems such as central vacuum systems, wall and ceiling speakers inside and outside, audio visual cableing, security and any other hidden systems. Town inspections are now needed for Mechanical, Plumbing, Electrical, Fire and then after all of these pass, rough framing is inspected. Now, we pick up the pace again!

At this point in the project, perform a careful walk through of the mechanical, electrical, and plumbing systems that are in place. It is much

less expensive to change anything at this point rather than after insulation and gypsum board are installed. Understand what switches operate which lights, make sure you have everything that you requested and don't forget to think about blocking (reinforcing in the walls) for items such as coat hook, towel bars and toilet paper holders.

When all these inspections are passed, it is time to start closing up the walls. Insulation in the roof, walls, and floor is installed and inspected, and you are ready for Gypsum Board (commonly referred to as sheetrock).

The Gypsum Board gets installed rather quickly and all joints and corners are taped and spackled with 3 coats and sanded smooth to be ready for painting. This is a messy step with lots of dust, so of this is a renovation, make sure the existing areas are well protected from the dust. When the sanding is completed the ceilings and walls should be wiped down to remove excess dust and then the entire place vacuumed to clear all of the dust.

The house looks so different at this point as it went from wide open rooms and walls that you could see through to what feels like smaller rooms.

Flooring is the next item to be installed. Hardwood flooring and tile are installed first and any carpet areas are saved until the end of the project. Confirm flooring size and layout and color prior to installation and do the same with tile, so there are no mistakes as to which rooms get which

materials. Verify patterns, grout colors, where accent tiles will be placed, the height to which wall tiles will be run, border locations, and base tile conditions at the walls. It's much simpler to go through each room and verify everything than to have to change it later. Take the time here that is needed.

Example of wood and Tile floors.

Interior Doors are installed now as well as cabinetry, windows, door base and trim. Ceiling trims, coffer ceiling details, and wall wainscoting would also all be installed at this stage. Railings and handrails are put in place at this time and you are ready for painting!

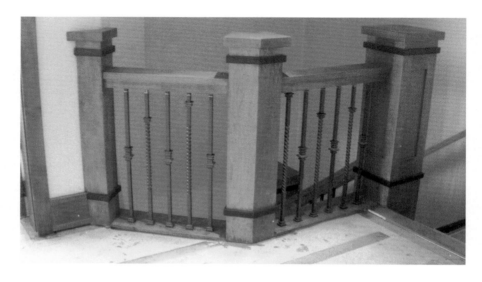

Note: If your hardwood floors are to be finished (sanded and stained onsite vs a prefinished material) then typically the sanding, staining, and 2 finish coats will be completed at this point, prior to painting and the final finish flow coat will be installed after painting.

The quality of paint jobs varied wildly depending on what you spend on this part of the job. Invest in a good painter! The biggest difference in quality will be the preparation work that is done prior to painting. Good quality painters will take the time to sand all of the trim smooth, fill nail holes and sand then and caulk all joints. After the primer coat is installed, they will sand the trim again to make sure it is smooth and ready for the 2 finish coats. Walls should be primed, any touch up spackling completed and sanded and then 2 top coats can be installed.

Wow – you are so close to a completed project! Interior door hardware and accessories such as towel bars, shower doors, toilets and appliances are installed. Ceiling and wall lights can be completed and then carpeting in rooms.

Now with everything completed, all of your final inspections should be scheduled and when these are all passed, the final Certificate of Occupancy (referred to as a C.O.) can be applied for and obtained.

The decorating portion of the design would begin at this time with drapes and shades being hung, area rugs and furniture delivered and all sub-systems – TVs, speakers, etc hung and confirmed operational.

The exterior landscaping, pathways, and driveway will typically be started after installation of Gypsum board. Landscaping and exterior touches can be finalized as trim and painting are finished up inside.

So what happens if there are items that you notice that are not quite to your liking? Perhaps a wall has a scratch in it, a door handle does not operate smoothly, a window screen is ripped? These are called Punchlist items and you should do a walk through with your General Contractor and make a detailed room by room punchlist so there are no misunderstandings about what is expected.

Remember, it is all about clear communication. Every job has punchlist items that need to be corrected or finished up, but if you stay on top of the project at each phase, it will minimize the items that need to be addressed at completion.

Voila! Your masterpiece is complete! It is certainly an exciting journey and when you move in, it is so worth it!

Before

This waterfront home was altered, an addition put on, and lifted up. The owner had a strong emotional connection to the original house. The parents had built it so care was taken to preserve that portion. Keeping in touch with the owner and builder through the entire process resulted in a very happy client for PDRdesigns.

After

14 INSPECTIONS

In the previous chapter, I touched on when different town inspections are required. In this chapter I will explain the purpose of inspections, who is responsible for them and what to do if you don't pass an inspection.

Inspections are performed by town, country or state inspectors, depending on the situation. These are done in order to ensure your house is built according to the proper building codes and that it will be a safe structure for your family as well as any future family that mat occupy the house. I have had clients that ask if a code can be not adhered to and they will sign a waiver accepting responsibility. This is not allowed as your structure must be safe and code confirming for any future inhabitants as well.

Your General Contractor is responsible for making sure all inspections are scheduled and passed before continuing with the next construction stage. My recommendation to you is to find out what inspections are required and request a copy of the passed sticker for each one completed. This way you can confirm how the project is going and that everything is being done correctly. Each town or governing agency will provide a list of inspections needed and it varies from region to region and town to town. Here is a list of common inspections and when they occur.

Footing – This is done after footings are dug and reinforcing installed

Foundation Wall – If doing a poured wall, then it will be inspected after the forms are up and reinforcing installed or if block walls with reinforcing, they need to be inspected prior to filling the block cores with concrete.

Foundation Location – This is done after the foundation is complete and a surveyor verifies it is on the correct location and height.

Slab – if electrical or plumbing are under a basement or house slab, they would be inspected first and then the slab inspection done.

Sheathing Inspection – Performed after the house is framed and Exterior Plywood (sheathing) is installed. This ensures the nails are installed at the correct spacing in the sheathing. Windows also need to be installed for this so their installation can be inspected.

Rough Electrical – Done after framing is complete and all electrical and low voltage wiring is completed.

Rough Plumbing – After all framing is complete and plumbing pipes installed and shower pans and tubs filled with water to make sure there are no leaks.

Rough Fire – Done after electrical and plumbing. This makes sure all fire blocking and caulking is completed correctly.

Rough Framing – After above inspections are passed, this verifies all framing is installed correctly and accurately.

Insulation – Verifies the correct R-valve rating and installation techniques for insulation is done.

Gypsum Board – Verifies correct nailing patterns are used on the installed gypsum board.

Final Electrical – When all electrical systems are installed, finished, and operational.

Final Plumbing – When all plumbing fixtures are installed, finished, and operational.

Final Fire – When all smoke detectors and mechanical and venting systems are operational.

Final Building – After all previous inspections are passed. This verifies all items are completed correctly and according to the Architectural Plans.

So with all of these inspections, what happens when they don't pass you? The one inspector will give you a list of the specific items and their locations that are not code compliant and then the subcontractor that did the work is responsible for correcting it and obtaining the new passing inspections.

Keep an eye on progress, make sure all inspections are passed along the way and relax knowing you have the knowledge to understand the process!

15 THE HOLY GRAIL – CERTIFICATE OF OCCUPANCY

A house is made of walls and beams, a home Is built with love and dreams.

— Dr. William A. Ward

Why would I refer to the Certificate of Occupancy as the Holy Grail and what is it?

The Certificate of Occupancy, often referred to as the C.O. or C of O is what the town issues after all construction is complete, inspections passed and applicable paperwork filed and fees paid. It tells you that everything has been completed correctly and now you may move into your new home or addition.

I jokingly call it the Holy Grail because everyone sought the Holy Grail in the old days and when building, the item that everyone seeks in the Certificate of Occupancy. All the work that is done leading up to being able to obtain the C.O. at the end, which marks the end of the project. This also is the point where Banks will convert construction loans into a mortgage and issue final payments.

As discussed in the Inspections chapter everything must be completed and inspected correctly all along the way to obtain this. I recommend getting a list from the Building Department early on in the process as to what is required to have the C.O issued. Some jurisdictions will have simpler requirements than others.

I recently helped a couple that was having difficulties obtaining the C.O. They had acted as their own General Contractor during the project and thought when the final inspection was passed that they automatically received the C.O. They did not realize there was a list of items to submit, verify and pay for prior to obtaining the C.O. for that town. No one had told them and they didn't know enough to ask. It is for clients such as this that I write this book, as it will make the process easier when you understand what is required.

When you finally obtain your Certificate of Occupancy take a moment to relax, have a drink to celebrate and begin enjoying your wonderful new home!

Sometimes it is necessary to obtain a Temporary Certificate of Occupancy (T.C.O.). This may not be offered by all towns and will have different requirements, but the basic difference is the T.C.O. may be issued after all inspections are completed and the town agrees that the construction portion is complete and done correctly. There may be additional paperwork that is still needed for a full C.O. but the T.C.O. will allow you to move into your new home. This may help with getting you out of a rental or selling your existing home.

16 WARRANTIES

In the end, you have to protect yourself at all times.

— Floyd Mayweather Jr.

When deciding what General Contractor will be building your project, find out what warranties they offer. Typically, there is a one year labor warranty on all work completed, which means if an item was installed wrong and starts to fall apart, the General Contractor will come back and fix it at no charge. Find out what their policy is up front.

As items get installed in your house, make sure your contractor gives you a copy of the owner's manual with the install date, Model # and Serial # clearly written on it. This will assist you if anything breaks down while still under warranty (although it seems like items break down about a week after the warranty expires).

When you build a new home, you will receive a Homeowner's Warranty which is purchased through the state, if your state has this program in place.

A great contractor will provide each client a binder with all of the details and information for every piece of the house. Beautiful work and a great idea to keep their clients happy!

17 CONFLICT RESOLUTION

Communication is the key to a well designed and built project. When communication gets off track, this is when conflict resolution is needed.

Conflict Resolution does not have to mean going to court. It can be as simple as sitting down at a table and discussing a topic. The easiest Conflict Resolution is to spot an issue early and address it CLEARLY! The most common cause of conflicts is a misunderstanding of expectations, whether they are quality, time, or cost related. Let's use an example: You, the owner arrive at the jobsite at the end of every day. Do you call your contractor and vent or ask him to meet you onsite to tell him what you expected or what you do expect going forward. (Let me give you a tip here. In my experience, the cheaper the cost, the messier the jobs site).

Your next step is to send an email stating as per our discussion today, it was agreed that the jobsite will be clean and neat at the end of every day. This way if there is an issue again, you have a record of it and can determine your next best course of action. This is a minor issue, but the same principals apply to other conflicts.

The most common issue is time delays. This stems from contractors not doing what they have said they would or owners not making decisions in a timely manner. You should ask for a written schedule up front as to when the various phases will begin or be completed and what decisions from you they are dependent upon. This way you know what is expected of you.

If you see the project is not going as scheduled, sit down with the contractor to discuss it or get you architect included to help resolve why and how to correct it moving forward. If the schedule is way behind to the point you feel they are not giving your job enough attention and you have addressed this in writing a few times, then it may be time for an attorney letter.

The next step if they continue to delay the job would be to remove them from the project, but consult your attorney before doing this so that you understand your rights and follow the correct procedures. Here is an excellent example of why you should not use the contractor that is crazy low in price. Quality and Time will be sacrificed and if you have to remove them, you will need to find someone to complete the project. This can be expensive as you may have already paid this contractor too much money and now you have to pay a premium to get another contractor in to fix a job or pick up the pieces and continue.

"The Quality of our lives depends not on whether or not we have conflicts, but on how we respond to them."

— Tom Crum

Years ago, I designed a 2nd floor addition for a lovely couple and they based their price on a contractor that was a friend who was helping them. This was the largest job he had ever done. (Warning – lights should be flashing when you hear this from anyone)

The family was excited about the project and all smiles as it began. The roof was scheduled to be removed, the second floor framed and the project should have been water tight in 5 days. Framing dragged on a few extra days and when a storm came in, the project was covered with tarps but they were not secured properly and not installed to shed water correctly at all locations.

The house was leaking everywhere! The family was upset, but the contractor promised to fix it all. The family moved out, put their belongings into a storage container and hoped it would be ok (rent for housing and storage was not figured in the budget).

The contractor continued and replaced some sheetrock in a few places. The family did not monitor how it was fixed and assumed he did it correctly. About a month later, black mold was everywhere on the 1st floor, which was supposed to remain intact. Finally, distraught at this point, they contacted an attorney. The contractors insurance company was contacted, but all of the damage was due to faulty workmanship and that is specifically not covered in Contractors Insurance Policies!

The contractor was brought to court, sued, and the family won the case. However, the contractor had no savings, rented a house and had a small company with no assets. So although they won an award, there was no money to collect.

The financial loss was tremendous. Worse was the time and emotional trauma from having to go through all of that.

In the end, the entire house was gutted down to the studs, treated for mold and put back together. We discussed many framing problems with the work that was performed and these issues had to be corrected as well. I was not made aware of the problems until after the attorney was brought in. I did all that I could to help alleviate their anxiety.

This could have all been avoided had they hired a qualified contractor. They are still trying to pay off all of the unexpected expenses they incurred.

Qualify the contractor before hiring! Know how conflicts will be resolved, understand your rights and clearly communicate your expectations in writing. These steps will help to ensure a smooth project that you will enjoy and remember!

Peace is not the absence of conflict, but the ability to cope with it
— *Dorothy Thomas*

CONCLUSION

Summing up the entire process from <u>Architectural Design to Construction</u>, I will say its most important to be informed, understand the time frame for the project to unfold, and communicate frequently with all parties involved.

The most successful and enjoyable projects for me have been working with clients that understand the process and have realistic expectations. As I write this conclusion on a Saturday morning, I think of my client and now friend, Ken. Ken had a unique project and as the design process unfolded we came up with creative solutions. Ken had done renovations before and knows a bit about what to expect. What he didn't know we educated him about and now as the construction is in full swing, nothing has come up that he wasn't prepared for. This has led to a happy client who thanks us for the guidance and input, which has led him to him being able to Enjoy the Process and I know soon he will Love the Outcome!

This reminds me of one of my favorite clients, Dave and Kristin from a few years ago who had a very challenging house which we were able to turn into a beautiful home that thrilled them. We were with them every step of the way and I was thrilled when they were sitting on their deck talking about how the project had gone and decided to call me right away to thank me! What an amazing feeling to know that we have touched and enhanced our client's lives!

Before

Dave and Kristin's house, mentioned above transformed from an eyesore to a refreshing beautiful home!

After

It is my hope that the knowledge that this book has provided to you will make your next project fun, exciting, and smooth. If you have any questions along the way, reach out to my office and we will guide you along your journey! My goal is that from Architectural Design through Construction and everything that happens in between, you will...

Create Your Dreams...

Enjoy the Process...

Love the Outcome!

ADDITIONAL RESOURCES

- Sample Architectural Agreement
- Sample Cost Spreadsheet
- Folder Categories for Organizing
  - Architectural Design
  - Interior Design
  - Contracts/Invoices
  - Material Selections
  - Plumbing Fixtures
  - Lighting Fixtures
  - Technology
  - Permits
  - Landscaping
  - Warranties/Manuals
- Recommended Design Idea Websites
  - Houzz
    - www.houzz.com
  - Pinterest

- ☐ www.pinterest.com
  - o Google Images
    - ☐ www.google.com
- Professional Recommendation Websites
  - o Porch
    - ☐ www.porch.com
  - o Angie's List
    - ☐ www.angieslist.com
  - o AIA (American Institute of Architects)
    - ☐ www.aia.org
  - o NARI (National Association of the Remodeling Industry)
    - ☐ www.nari.org
  - o NAHB (National Association of Home builders)
    - ☐ www.nahb.org

ARCHITECTURE

501 Laurel Ave. Suite 4, Point Pleasant Beach, NJ 08742

Phone (732) 703-3799	www.PDRdesigns.com
Fax (732) 367-7223	Email Paul@PDRdesigns.com

ARCHITECTURAL AGREEMENT

Date

Client Name
Client Address
City State Zip

Dear Name

It was a pleasure speaking with you regarding Architectural Design Services for your home project. To complete this project, my firm will bring over 50 combined years of architectural and construction experience to help you create your design. My understanding of the project requirements from our discussions is as follows:

- Scope of Work

The Stages for this project are as follows:

Stage 1: Documenting Existing Conditions – Measuring all existing buildings, floor plans and elevations in order to establish a beginning point for all renovations and addition projects. (Your surveyor will perform site measurements)

Stage 2: Discovery and Programming
Discovery – Evaluating the current building site including zoning and code research
Programming – Identifying the homeowner's needs and wants and together establishing a clear scope of the work to be completed.

Stage 3: Schematic Design – Creating rough sketches for the client as a beginning point for discussion. This stage is about traffic flow through the house and site and functional relationships. Since design is a fluid process, nothing is hard lined at this point. It may take 1 or 2 more iterations before the Client approves the schematic design and moves to the next phase.

Client name

Stage 4: Design Development – Refining the rough sketches into plans, elevations and detailed drawings. Materials and mechanical systems will be discussed during this stage. These drawings will form the basis for the construction documents and will be approved by the owner before moving forward. This is the time we like to identify consultants to include on the project team. At PDRdesigns, we believe that best projects are the result of the combined efforts of the Client, Architect, Designers, and Contractors. (The architect can make recommendations for a qualified contractor)

Stage 5: Construction Documents – Providing detailed documents so that building permits can be obtained by the General Contractor. All jurisdictions require a code compliant set of documents to issue a building permit. We work with you and your contractor to ensure that you are able to obtain your permits.

Measure Existing Conditions:	\$.00/ sq ft
The investment for these services will be done on an hourly basis as detailed below:	
Architectural Draftsman	\$ per hour
Architectural Associate	\$ per hour
Project Architect:	\$ per hour
Retainer due upon signing of agreement:	**\$**

A copy of the survey and soil boring are required in order to start the project. In addition, homes within a flood hazard area will require a flood elevation certificate.

Progress billing to be completed every two weeks based on work completed.

All prints needed for meetings, variances, building department submittals or other purposes will be charged at a rate of \$6.00 per sheet for black and white sheets.

Any requests for prints to be mailed will be billed as per USPS or FEDEX postage rates.

The timeframe for this project will be dictated by the owner's decisions and the number of revisions to the plans.

Additional Services we can provide:

Building Rendering – a 3-D perspective of the finished house:

- This item allows clients to see the finished product and is extremely helpful for those that cannot visualize the spaces from the architectural blueprints.

Soil Boring and Geotechnical Analysis:
*(Please provide a copy of your soil boring. If you do not have a soil boring, we can provide that service for you)

- This item is for the footing analysis and verification and can be provided by us or your site engineer.

Client name
PDRdesigns

Additional Notes:

- All local zoning requirements and setbacks will be reviewed with the site engineer. Site engineering and surveying will need to be contracted separately.
- Electrical, Plumbing, Heating and Cooling systems will all be reviewed in the construction document phase.
- There may be concealed conditions that are uncovered during the normal course of construction that could not be anticipated and will require additional input from the architect as an additional service.

Terms and Conditions:

1. Insurance rates may be affected by decisions made by the owner during the design process. The architect is not responsible for insurance rates and regulations.
2. Any change to building codes during the design process may require additional work and will be considered an additional service..
3. If project design begins prior to architect having an updated site plan, then the owner takes responsibility for and agrees to compensate architect and consultants as necessary for any and all work required for redesign due to zoning issues.
4. Any variances or board approval filings are not a part of this contract.
5. Alterations requested by the owner after the preliminary design is approved will be considered an additional service.
6. The architect is not responsible for construction costs, but recommends budgeting $200/sq. ft. for construction costs for altered and new construction.
7. All outstanding balances are due within 7 days of the invoice date.
8. Any modifications made during construction or deviation from the final Construction Documents must be relayed to the Architect's office for approval, prior to undertaking a change.
9. Dispute resolution, if required, will be performed by Benchmark Resolution Services LLC, located in Brick, NJ, and judgment on the award rendered by the arbitrator may be entered in any court having jurisdiction thereof.
10. As per Federal Copyright Law, all architectural preliminary and final designs remain the property of PDRdesigns LLC. PDF copies of the drawings will be provided to the owner for their use on this building site only.
11. A jobsite sign will be allowed to be installed on the property advertising PDRdesigns LLC for the duration of the project.
12. The owners agree to allow PDRdesigns to take pictures of the project for use in advertising media; however no names or addresses will be used in conjunction with the photographs.
13. Signed and Sealed Construction Documents will not be released until final payment is received.

Client name
PDRdesigns

14. Architectural drawings are to be submitted to the building department for construction permits. It is the owners' responsibility to ensure permits are obtained prior to beginning construction.

Please sign and return one copy of this Agreement with the retainer check, made payable to PDRdesigns, LLC.

Thank you for the opportunity to be of service to you. If you have any questions, you can reach me at (732) 703-3799. I am looking forward to working with you on this project!

We will exceed your expectations!

SIGNED: _____ DATE: _____

Paul David Rugarber, AIA
NJ License #AI14158
NY License #035085

SIGNED: _____ DATE: _____

Client Name

Additional Services (if requested):

Building Rendering – a 3-D perspective of the house:

SIGNED: _____ DATE: _____

Soil Boring and Geotechnical Analysis:

SIGNED: _____ DATE: _____

Client name
PDRdesigns

PDR DESIGNS LLC				
Sample Cost Spreadsheet				
ITEM	MATERIAL	LABOR	SUBCONTRACTOR COST	TOTAL
General Conditions				
Job Supervisor / Project Manager				
Survey, stakeout, certifications				
Building Permits				
Temporary Electric				
Temporary Water				
Temporary Toilet				
Dumpsters / Cleanup				
Floor Protection				
Final Cleaning				
Sitework - Water & Sewer Connections / Backfill				
Paver Driveway & Walks				
Landscaping				
Pool				
Demolition of Existing House & Foundation				
Pilings (if required)				
Concrete Footings and Foundation Walls				
Structural Steel beams and columns				
Exterior Waterproofing				
Rough Carpentry - Framing & Installation of Exterior windows and doors				
Deck Framing				
Finish carpentry: trim-base, casing, door installation, crown, columns				
Roofing				
Metal Roofing				
Exterior siding and trim				

ITEM	MATERIAL	LABOR	SUBCONTRACTOR COST	TOTAL
PDR DESIGNS LLC				
Sample Cost Spreadsheet				
Lightning Protection System				
Fiberglass Decks				
Windows & Exterior Doors (Material)				
Entry Door System (Material) and Installation				
Interior Doors (Material)				
Interior Door Hardware				
Overhead Garage Doors				
Interior Stairs & Railings				
Insulation				
Attic Stairs				
Gypsum Board				
Hardwood Floors				
Carpet				
Tile floors, walls, backsplash				
Painting & Staining				
Kitchen Cabinets and countertops				
Appliances				
Central Vacuum System				
Security System				
Exterior Decking, Rails, and Columns				
Bathroom Vanities and Hardware				
Vanity Tops				
Built-In Cabinetry and Hardware				
Shower Doors				
Closet shelves, rods or cabinets				

			PDR DESIGNS LLC		
			Sample Cost Spreadsheet		
ITEM	MATERIAL	LABOR	SUBCONTRACTOR COST	TOTAL
Bath Accessories - Mirrors, Towel Bars, Toilet Paper Holder				
Plumbing Fixtures & Hardware				
HVAC - Heating Ventillation, and Air conditioning				
Audio visual -Phone, cable, data, speakers, T.V.				
Lighting Fixtures				
Electrical				
Subtotal				
Overhead & Profit @ 20%				
TOTAL PRICE				
Building Square Footage		Price / SF =		

ABOUT THE AUTHOR

Walking along the beach at the Jersey Shore you notice the boundless ocean on one side and the gorgeous homes on the other. This is Paul's world! His weekends are spent coaching soccer and hockey games for his 4 kids or on the rare occurrence relaxing at the beach. Chopping wood, walking with his dog, Reeces, and skiing in the winter are a few of his other hobbies.

Mention Paul's favorite teams the NJ Devils or the Pittsburgh Steelers and his eyes light up. Paul is a brown belt in karate and has run the Dublin Marathon but currently enjoys staying fit with his Beachbody Coaching.

Being an avid reader and always wanting to encourage and motivate others, Paul uses his talents and knowledge by coaching other professionals in helping them reach their potential. He begins each day sharing a smile and motivational quote with his team. Staying upbeat and positive is their office culture.

You can view his motivational videos and quotes on YouTube, Facebook, and Instagram where he enjoys sharing them with others (or possibly he just likes to hear himself talk).

Some of his community involvement includes being the past President of the Jersey Shore Toastmasters, President of the Jackson Liberty Ice Hockey Board, and Jackson Planning Board member.

Paul is super proud of his Architectural Firm, being named the American Institute of Architects Jersey Shore Firm of the Year for 2017!

He would love to have you visit him at his office in downtown Point Pleasant Beach and have lunch with him at Joe Leone's Italian Specialties right next door.

You can reach Paul directly at 732-703-3799 or stop into his office at 501 Laurel Ave. Suite 4, Point Pleasant Beach, NJ 08742.

As a father, Architect, Speaker and now Author, he hopes that you enjoy this book and he looks forward to meeting you sometime soon!

God Bless,

Paul David Rugarber
Architect of Life

Made in the USA
Middletown, DE
18 January 2019